Collins

Easy Learning

KS3 English Revision

Levels 3–5

Kim Richardson

About this book

This book has been written to help you prepare for your Key Stage 3 English test at the end of Year 9. It contains all the content you need to do well in the reading, writing and Shakespeare papers.

The book is divided into three sections corresponding to the three papers. Each topic is contained within a double page. The left-hand page has all the information and the right-hand page has an annotated example, a sample question and/or an answer to show how the information can be applied in the test.

The sample answers have been given approximate National Curriculum levels and/or a comment for guidance, so you can see the level of the answer and compare it to your own.

Special features

- **Spot Check questions** on every double page are a quick way to check that you've taken in the key points. You can find the answers to these on the inside back cover.

- **Top Tips** pick out some key techniques to help you raise your level.

- **Cross-references** show pages where you can find more information about a particular point.

> Page 26 (formal language). →

- **Did You Know?** items are there just for fun and a bit of light relief.

Revision and practice

Use this book alongside Collins *Easy Learning KS3 English Workbook Levels 3–7*. The workbook contains test-style questions and practice papers so you can check that you have learnt and understood everything from this revision book.

Published by Collins
An imprint of HarperC
77 – 85 Fulham Palac
Hammersmith
London W6 8JB

Browse the complete
www.collins.co.uk

© HarperCollins*Publish*

10 9 8 7 6 5 4

ISBN-13 978-0-00-723
ISBN-10 0-00-723353-

Kim Richardson asserts his moral right to be identified as the author of this work.

All rights reserved. No part of this publication may be reproduced, stored in a retrieval system, or transmitted in any form or by any means, electronic, mechanical, photocopying, recording or otherwise, without the prior written permission of the Publisher or a licence permitting restricted copying in the United Kingdom issued by the Copyright Licensing Agency Ltd., 90 Tottenham Court Road, London W1T 4LP.

British Library Cataloguing in Publication Data
A Catalogue record for this publication is available from the British Library.

Written by Kim Richardson
Edited by Sue Chapple
Design by Sally Boothroyd
Illustrations by Fliss Cary, Linzie Hunter, Andy Tudor, David Whittle, Sue Woollatt
Index compiled by Jane Read
Printed and bound in Malaysia by Imago

Acknowledgements
The Publishers gratefully acknowledge the following for permission to reproduce copyright material:
Extract from *Follow Me Down* by Julie Hearn (OUP, 2003), copyright © Julie Hearn 2003, reprinted by permission of Oxford University Press.
Extract from inside panel entitled 'Protecting ancient forests' in 'Do you share our passion?' Greenpeace leaflet, www.greenpeace.org.uk. Reprinted with permission.
'Death of the Ladette' by Laura Neill, in the *Daily Star*, 10 November 2005. Reprinted with permission.
Extract from *RACE AGAINST TIME* by Ellen MacArthur (Michael Joseph, 2005) Copyright © Ellen MacArthur, 2005.
Reprinted with permission of A P Watt Ltd on behalf of Offshore Challenges Ltd
Adapted from review of *Imperial Glory* by Lee Hall, in *BBC Focus Magazine*, August 2005. Reprinted with permission.
Extract from p. 41 of *Stone Cold* by Robert Swindells, published by Hamish Hamilton, 1993. Copyright © Robert Swindells, 1993. Reproduced with permission of Penguin Books Ltd.
'Weatherwatch' by Kate Ravilious, in *The Guardian*, 30 November 2005. Copyright Guardian Newspapers Limited 2005. Reprinted with permission.

Photographs
The Author and Publishers are grateful to the following for permission to reproduce photographs:
p. 15 Frans Lanting/Corbis
p. 17 HELLESTAD RUNE/CORBIS SYGMA
p. 19 Reuters/CORBIS
p. 35 Richard Cummins/CORBIS
p. 83, 91 Donald Cooper/photostage.co.uk

Whilst every effort has been made to trace the copyright holders, in cases where this has been unsuccessful, or if any have inadvertently been overlooked, the Publishers will be pleased to make the necessary arrangements at the first opportunity.

Contents

Answers to Spot Check questions
are on the inside back cover.

The Key Stage 3 tests

What are the Key Stage 3 tests?

- In Year 9 you will be taking national tests in three subjects – English, Maths and Science. Everyone across the country will take the same tests.

- There are three papers in the English test: reading, writing and Shakespeare.

The reading paper

- The reading test lasts 1 hour and 15 minutes. The first 15 minutes of this is simply to read a booklet which contains three extracts.

- All the extracts are on the same topic (e.g. animals, or sport), but they will be written in very different styles.

- You will be tested on how well you understand the extracts and how well you can comment on their language, structure and purpose.

The writing paper

- The writing test lasts 1 hour and 15 minutes. It contains two writing tasks.

- In Section A (45 minutes) you do one long piece of writing. You are given 15 minutes to plan this piece of writing.

- In Section B (30 minutes) you do a shorter piece of writing.

- You will be tested on how well you can write. This includes the way you organise your answers. Some marks are given for grammar, punctuation and spelling.

The Shakespeare paper

- The Shakespeare test lasts 45 minutes. You are given one question about the play you have been studying in class.

- You will be given a booklet which contains the question and the extracts from the play that you have been studying.

- You will be tested on your understanding of the extracts, and how well you can comment on them.

Speaking and listening

- Skills in speaking and listening are an important part of the English curriculum. These skills are assessed by your teacher. The assessment is based on work that you have done in class over the year. Speaking and listening are not assessed in the national tests.

What happens then?

- Your test papers are sent away to be marked by outside examiners.

- You will be awarded a National Curriculum level between 3 and 7 for your work across all three papers. The expected level for 14-year-olds is level 5. You should aim for at least a level 5.

Top Tip!

- Things you should take with you:
  Two pens (in case one runs out) ✓
  A highlighter pen, to mark bits in the passages ✓
  A brain full of energy and ideas ✓
- Things you should not take with you:
  A dictionary ✗
  Your Shakespeare play ✗
  A tired head and an empty stomach ✗

Did You Know?

Although you (and your teacher) probably call them the Year 9 SATs, their proper name is the Key Stage 3 tests.

Spot Check

Discuss in groups the best ways that you have of:
1 planning your revision
2 practising English skills
3 remembering facts (for the Shakespeare paper)
4 handling stress

READING — The reading paper

The key things you need to know

- The reading test lasts 1 hour and 15 minutes. It is worth 32 marks.

- You are given a **reading booklet**, which contains three texts (extracts).

- You are also given an **answer booklet**, which contains about 12 questions on the texts. You write your answers in the space provided.

The texts

- The three texts will all be new to you. They will be on the same **topic** (e.g. animals), but they will be written in very different **styles**.

- They will normally include fiction and non-fiction texts. The non-fiction texts will be in different **forms**, e.g. book extract, newspaper report, interview, leaflet … all sorts.

- The texts will have different **purposes**, e.g. to explain, to tell a story, to persuade an audience, to review a film.

Pages 8, 12, 16, 20, 24 (different types of text).

Reading time

- The first 15 minutes is **reading time**. You use this time to read the texts in the reading booklet.

- Do *not* read the questions during the reading time. Just read the three texts carefully.

- As you read, you can highlight or underline any **key words or phrases**. Also, try to notice **key features** of the texts, such as their structure, how language is used and the mood or tone of the writing.

Pages 10, 14, 18, 22, 26 (key features).

- You don't need to remember everything in the texts. You will be able to re-read the important bits when you answer the questions.

The questions

There are about four questions on each text. The questions will be of **different types**.

- Some questions will be short, and only give you 1 mark each. Others will be longer, and may give you up to 5 marks.

- You may be asked to write a word, a sentence or a paragraph. You may be asked to tick a box, fill in a table or complete a sentence.

- The questions may ask you to:
  - **find information**
  - **comment** on language or structure
  - give your **opinion**
  - **explain** the writer's **viewpoint and purpose**.

Pages 28–37 (answering different types of question).

Answering the questions

- Start at the beginning and work your way through the questions in order. The first few questions refer to the first text in the reading booklet, and so on.

- **Do exactly what you are asked.** For example, if you are asked to write a word or phrase, don't write an essay.

- Look at the **marks** given for each question, and the **space** provided in the answer booklet. They will give you an idea about how much you should write.

Top Tip!

You will be tested on:
- whether you answer the **precise** question ✓
- how well you understand and can comment on the texts ✓

You will *not* be tested on:
- your writing style ✗
- your spelling, punctuation or grammar ✗

Timing

- You have 1 hour to answer all the questions. That means about 20 minutes for the questions on each text.

- Use the **marks** as a guide. You shouldn't spend more than 2 minutes per mark.

- Leave 5 minutes at the end to **read through and check** your answers.

Spot Check

Look at these questions. What type of answer is each question asking for? **a** giving your opinion, **b** finding information, **c** commenting on language.
1 Which words show that Sam is frightened?
2 Comment on the writer's use of language to describe how frightened Sam is.
3 What do you think Sam is most frightened of in this passage?

What is fiction?

- Fiction means **stories**. Common forms are short stories and novels (longer stories).

- Fiction describes imaginary events in a way that entertains the reader.

- The key features of a story to comment on are the **plot**, **language**, **setting** and **characters**.

Pages 10–11 (characters).

Plot

- The plot is the **storyline**. Plots often have an introduction, a development (build up), a crisis (when the story comes to a head) and a resolution (when things are sorted out).

- **Fast moving** plots are exciting and full of tension. **Slow moving** plots focus more on character, mood and description.

Language

- Words are chosen carefully to create a precise effect. Writers use **descriptive detail** and draw vivid pictures (**imagery**) as in this extract from the text opposite: *for a moment the page of the London A to Z he was supposed to be reading blurred and swam beneath his eyes.*

- Writers pay attention to the **structure** of their sentences. Notice the length of these sentences: *Quickly he knuckled the wet from his face. Had his mother noticed? If she had, he would say it was sweat. And that he felt sick.*

Setting

- The setting is the **place** and **time** in which the story is set.

- The way the author describes the setting contributes to the **mood** or **atmosphere** of the story. The extract opposite is set in a hot, smelly meat market. It helps to create a stifling, heavy atmosphere.

Spot Check

1 What are the four key features of stories?
2 Explain what the resolution of a story is.
3 Think about a novel or short story you have read. What is the plot?

Question

This is the opening passage from a novel.

List two things which are intended to grab the reader's interest.

> It was the stench seeping in through the car windows that bothered Tom the most. Rank and beefy, it reminded him of the way dogs smell after a walk in the rain. Smelly dogs made him think of Goldie, left behind in Dorset, and for a moment the page of the London *A to Z* he was supposed to be reading blurred and swam beneath his eyes.
>
> Quickly he knuckled the wet from his face. Had his mother noticed? If she had, he would say it was sweat. And that he felt sick. It was late morning, the middle of August, and hot enough for even a skinny twelve year old to be melting like a lolly. Add the stink of Smithfield meat market, leaching through traffic fumes, and anyone with nostrils and a stomach in working order was bound to feel bad.

(From *Follow Me Down*, by Julie Hearn)

Answer

1 The good description of the smell draws us in to the story. The author uses vivid and powerful language, for example the words 'stench' and 'rank and beefy', to make us feel we are really there.

2 The author implies that the boy is in London, but we want to know what he is doing there and why he has left his dog behind.

level 4

Top Tip!

To get a level 5 you need to be able to comment on how the writer **implies** (not just states) what is going on. That means reading between the lines.

Did You Know?

The author John Creasey wrote 565 books in 40 years. Twenty-six of them were written in a single year!

Characters

- **Believable** and **interesting** characters are central to the success of a story.

- Things happen to characters, but characters also **develop** (change) through a story.

- Characters affect each other. These **relationships** are often the key aspects of a story.

Top Tip!

To get a level 5 you need to be able to show that you understand what a character is **feeling**, not just what he or she is like.

Describing characters

You can learn about characters in different ways:

- by **how they look**, e.g. *He had small piercing eyes that were set too closely together.*

- by **how they speak**, e.g. *"Found a shilling, huh?" His voice was gruff. "Want to show me?"*

- by **what they do**, e.g. *He sidled up to me, then grabbed at my hand and sank his teeth into it.*

Dialogue

- Characters' speech is called **dialogue**.

- Dialogue can include different **accents** (pronunciation) and **dialect** (e.g. regional versions of speech).

- Each character will have their own way of speaking, which will be **consistent** through the story.

Narrative viewpoint

- The point of view from which the story is told is called the **narrative viewpoint**.

- A **1st person narrative** is written as if one of the characters is telling it, e.g. *I opened the package carefully.*

- A **3rd person narrative** is told by the author, e.g. *Nasreem opened the package carefully.*

Question

Read the extract on page 9 again.

What do we learn about the character Tom?

Answer

Tom is in a car. We know that because of the car windows in the first sentence. He's also in London, though he comes from Dorset, where his dog has been left behind – 'left behind in Dorset'.

We also learn that it is very smelly. This is because of the meat market, which they must be driving through or near. It makes him feel really bad. In fact it 'bothered Tom the most'.

Tom is also very hot, it is August. He's twelve years old and skinny.

level
5

Comment

This is a level 5 answer because it covers the main points that we are told about Tom. It also shows some understanding of Tom, including his feeling of being bothered by the smell. This point is backed up by a relevant quotation from the text.

The answer would gain a higher level if it mentioned Tom's sadness (rather than focusing on the dog), as well as his attempt to hide his feelings from his mother. More detailed and relevant reference to the text would also add marks.

Spot Check

1 What is a 1st person narrative?
2 Name three ways in which an author can show what a character is like.
3 What is the difference between accent and dialect?

Reading texts that persuade, argue, advise

Purpose and audience

Some texts try to get the reader to do something, e.g. buy a product or agree with the writer's point of view. For example:

* Adverts may try to **persuade** you to buy an iPod.

* Newspaper articles may **argue** that footballers get paid too much.

* Health leaflets and magazine articles may **advise** you on how to eat properly.

Top Tip!

When commenting on an extract, remember to think about why it has been written. Point out how the words and layout suit the writer's **purpose**.

Structure

* The writing is usually presented as a series of points in a **logical order**.

* The **first sentence** in a paragraph or advert often makes the main point.

* Particular **words and phrases** are used to show how the points are connected or developed, e.g. *however, another point is …, in addition, on the other hand.*

* There is usually a powerful **opening** and **ending**.

Rhetorical techniques

Rhetorical techniques help get the message across effectively. Here are some examples:

* **Repetition**, e.g. *Let there be justice for all. Let there be peace for all.*

* Using 'you' to address the audience directly, and 'we' to include the audience on the writer's side.

* **Sound effects**, e.g. alliteration (*nuisance neighbours*) and rhyme (*a bad law, not a mad law*).

* **Emotive language** – language designed to make the audience feel something strongly, e.g. *They are destroying children's lives.*

Design and layout

Adverts and leaflets need to be **attractive** and **easy to read**. They may include:

- **Pictures** In an advert the picture may be very important.

- **Columns** The text is often in columns to make it easy to read.

- **Design** Colour, font style and size, use of bold/italic, graphics – all help to get the message across.

- **Subheadings** They break up the text into sections and guide the reader.

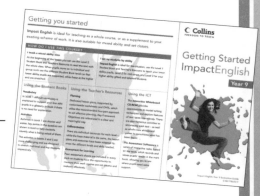

Example

Look at this example of a typical advice text:

Understanding the reader's problems/fears

Question to draw reader in

Worried about getting spots? The best thing is to eat a healthy balanced diet. It's not too difficult – you just need to:
- *have at least 5 portions of fruit and veg every day*
- *eat starchy foods, such as potatoes and rice*
- *go easy on the dairy products, such as cheese and milk.*

Addresses reader directly

Verbs tell reader what to do

Bullet point list to make points easy to follow

Conversational (informal) tone

Did You Know?

The first advert on TV was for Gibbs toothpaste, in 1955. The slogan was, "It's tingling fresh. It's fresh as ice. It's Gibbs SR toothpaste."

Spot Check

1 What is the purpose of an advert?
2 Give two ways in which adverts achieve their purpose.
3 Why do texts that persuade, argue or advise often begin with a question?

Fact

A **fact** is something that **can be proved** to be true:

- *Peter Jackson's film 'King Kong' was made in 2005.*

- *Wayne Rooney is a footballer.*

If people don't agree, you can check facts and show them the evidence.

Opinion

An **opinion** is someone's **point of view**:

- *'King Kong' was a fabulous film.*

- *Rooney's shot was unstoppable.*

These opinions cannot be proved to be true. They are the beliefs or judgements of the writer.

Where you find opinions

Opinions are found in all sorts of writing, e.g.

- **reviews** – where the reviewer gives their opinion about a film, CD or book

- **adverts** – where the audience is persuaded to agree with an opinion about a product

- **newspaper** and **magazine articles**, which argue for or against an opinion.

Persuasive opinions

Opinions can be very persuasive, so that you believe they are true:

- They can **disguise themselves as facts**, e.g. *Everyone knows that …*

- They can use **powerful words**, especially adjectives, e.g. *a perfect gift for Christmas* or *an appalling waste of money.*

- They can use **emotive language** e.g. *the holiday of your dreams* or *These men are preying on our children.*

Read this extract from a Greenpeace advert.

Give three examples of how the writer uses fact and opinion to persuade the reader to help the campaign.

fact – '80% of the world's ancient forests'. 80% is a lot.

opinion – LOVE. This word and the picture make you want to preserve the orang-utan.

Protecting ancient forests

A staggering 80% of the world's ancient forests have already been destroyed or degraded. Each year, millions of hectares of ancient forests are logged, often illegally, driven by international demand for cheap timber and other wood products, including paper. The UK is Europe's worst offender, with up to 50% of our tropical plywood coming from Indonesia's pristine rainforests. In Indonesia, an estimated 80% of the orang-utan's natural habitats have been wiped out in the last 20 years.

LOVE

opinion – 'The UK is Europe's worst offender'. It makes you want to stop your own country destroying forests.

Top Tip!

- To gain average marks you must **show the techniques** a writer has used to persuade the audience.
- To gain top marks you need to **explain how the writer has used** those techniques.

Did You Know?

It has been estimated that there are over a million words in the English language – over two million if all scientific terms are included.

**pot Check**

1 Are these facts or opinions?
  a It makes no difference if you skip breakfast.
  b Some people eat eggs and bacon for breakfast.
2 What is the effect of the emotive language used in this headline:

BUNNIES SLAUGHTERED IN THEIR THOUSANDS FOR FUR COATS

INFORMATION

Look out for these key features:

Purpose and audience

- **Information** texts include reference books, travel guides and leaflets.

- Their **purpose** is to give information about people, places and things.

- You read them to find out about something.

Structure

- Clear **organisation** and **logical order** of topics. **Subheadings** guide reader.

- **General statements** or **main points** first, then examples.

- **Tables** and **diagrams** might add information.

Language

- **Present tense** and **3rd person** (*he, she, it*) used.

- Clear, concise sentences.

- Usually **formal** English, and can include specialist words.

Top Tip!

If you are asked to comment on the layout of an information leaflet, think about the images, colours, font style and size, as well as how the images and writing work together.

RECOUNT

Look out for these key features:

Purpose and audience

- **Recount** texts include newspaper reports, travel writing and biography.

- Their **purpose** is to retell events.

- You read them to find out what happened, and often to be entertained.

Structure

- Events are generally told in **time order**.

- **Time connectives** guide the reader, e.g. *then* or *the following day*.

- New **paragraphs** mark a change of focus, such as a new time, place or person.

Language

- **Past tense**, though present tense may be used in newspaper stories.

- **Descriptive language** to bring events to life.

Page 18.

- Specific **details** given – dates, times, names, descriptions.

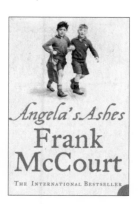

Articles in popular newspapers give information in a particular way:

Headline in full caps.

DEATH OF THE LADETTE
Old-fashioned girls don't want to party

Subheading tells you more about the subject of the article.

1st paragraph sums up the article.

Next few paragraphs give **more detail**.

Each **paragraph** is only one sentence.

Subheading used to catch eye and break up text.

Photos and **layout** important in popular newspaper stories.

■ by LAURA NEILL

BRITISH women are rejecting the ladette lifestyle for an old-fashioned family role.

They're turning their backs on the hard partying made famous by the likes of Sarah Cox, 31, and Zoe Ball, 34.

Instead the so-called 'new traditionalists' are married with children.

And they put the family before money and career, though they can combine both.

The new generation of 25 to 45-year-olds has been identified in a new survey.

They admire the values of their mother's era and believe in cooking and knitting, which has become trendy with the stars.

Twist

They snub food fads but know enough about health issues to realise what they should and shouldn't eat, according to the study for drinks firm Ovaltine.

Interviews with 500 women in the 25-45 age group found many wanted life to be 'more like the old days' with a modern twist.

Did You Know?

The book ...*All That Men Know About Women*, which was published in 1996, has 200 pages – but they're all blank!

 **Spot Check**

1 What is a biography?
2 'Diaries and autobiographies are written in the 1st person.' True or false?
3 What tense would you expect to be used in a description of the first moon landing?

Focus on: what makes a good description

Using the senses

- The senses are: looking, hearing, smelling, tasting and feeling. A good writer will make you use your senses:

  I felt my legs buckle beneath me. The ground rose up and hit me between my eyes. The earth didn't taste too good.

- A **visual image** is particularly important, as it lets the reader 'see' what is happening.

Imagery

Look out for these special ways of creating an image, or picture:

- **similes**, which compare something to something else, e.g. *Each harsh word was like the lash of a whip.*

- **metaphors**, which describe something as something else, e.g. *His body was a finely tuned machine which needed constant maintenance.*

- **personification**, which describes non-human things as if they were people, e.g. *The wind provided a helping hand as he cycled up the final hill.*

Top Tip!

Remember that a **simile** uses the words 'like' or 'as' to compare two things. A **metaphor** describes something directly as another thing.

Powerful words

- **Verbs** are 'doing' words. Precise or colourful verbs are very effective in passages describing action, e.g. *The eagle plummeted* (rather than 'dived'), *He hurled the book* (rather than 'threw').

- **Adjectives** are describing words, which usually go with nouns. They can make descriptions more vivid and detailed, e.g. *The piercing noise caused a frenzied squealing in the pig pens.*

**S**pot Check

What kind of imagery are these?
1 On the morning of my exam the sun rose reluctantly.
2 The flames of her hair crackled as she tossed her head.
3 He used his pen like a sword to attack his critics.

Read this email, which Ellen MacArthur sent on day 21 of her record-breaking voyage round the world.

Identify two things which make her description of the storm effective.

New Message

→ Send	✉ New	📎 Attach	🔍 Find	A Font	🖨 Print

To: [_____]

Subject: [_____]

Last night was a dark night, hard to see anything out there – nothing but the constant noise of B&Q[1] speeding through the water, the howling wind and the breaking of the waves. The waves are so steep here that poor B&Q feels like she's either running down a hill or being pushed hard up one. Waves regularly break on the windward float quarter. What is noticeable through the dark, shining brighter than our glowing instruments, are the crests of phosphorescence[2] – unbelievable, beautiful, and at times immense. We spend our time, even when trying to rest huddled in a ball in the cuddy[3], just feeling where we are on each mountain, how fast, how far and when will we hit the bottom …

[1]Ellen's boat
[2]tiny sea creatures that glow in the dark
[3]small sheltered area on board

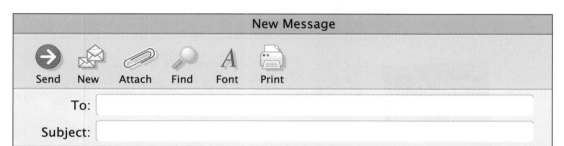

Answer

level 5

1 Ellen uses the senses. She makes us see things (the dark, then the glowing creatures) and hear things (the howling wind and breaking waves). She also tells us what she feels like in the last sentence.

2 Ellen also uses a metaphor – she describes the waves as hills, and later on as mountains.

Did You Know?

There are some unusual collective nouns in English, including an 'orchestra' of computers and a 'kindle' of kittens.

INSTRUCTION

Look out for these key features:

Purpose and audience

- **Instruction** texts include recipes, directions and DIY manuals.

- Their **purpose** is to tell you how to do something.

- You read one to find out how to do something.

Structure

- A series of step-by-step instructions in **time order**.

- May begin with a **list** of materials/ingredients needed.

- **Layout** makes the instructions easy to follow. May include diagrams, a numbered list, etc.

Language

- Uses **present tense**, **direct address** (you…) and **commands**, e.g. *Break six eggs into a bowl.*

- Written in **simple**, **clear sentences**, in formal English. Paragraphs are short.

- Includes **time connectives** to show the order you need to follow, e.g. *first* or *then*.

EXPLANATION

Look out for these key features:

Purpose and audience

- **Explanation** texts include science textbooks and letters explaining absence from school.

- Their **purpose** is to help someone understand how or why something happens, or how to do something.

- You read one to find out how something works, or how to do something.

Structure

- A series of **logical steps**.

- Each new point has a **new paragraph**.

- **Diagrams** or **illustrations** may help explain what to do.

Language

- **Present tense** used.

- **Connectives** guide the reader, e.g. *because* or *as a result* showing that one thing causes another. Time connectives, e.g. *next*, show the order.

- **Formal language**, e.g. *An electric current is generated by special muscle cells in the fish.* **Technical terms** may be used.

Page 26 (formal language).

Top Tip!

To gain a level 5 you need to be able to say **why** a text has been written (its purpose).

Note the key features of this instruction text. It is an extract from a recipe.

Clear format – a **numbered list**

1 Chop up a red cabbage and slice it thinly. Next, heat a saucepan of clean water until it boils.

2 Carefully add the cabbage to the boiling water. Then take the pan off the heat. Leave it to cool.

Time connectives

Sequence of points in chronological order. Each **paragraph** is a new point.

Direct address – note **commands**

Present tense and **short, simple sentences**

Did You Know?

The first English cookbook, 'Forme of Cury', was written in 1390 by the cooks of Richard II. These weren't curry recipes – 'cury' was the Old English word for 'cooking'!

 **Spot Check**

1 What kind of text are the rules of the card game Racing Demon?

2 Why do instructions use direct address?

3 What kind of connectives are 'then', 'next', 'the following day'?

Putting texts together

Structure refers to the way in which a text or passage is put together. This depends on its **purpose**:

- An **instruction** text is made up of a clear sequence of steps.

- An **argument** text may begin with the key point of view, then give reasons and evidence, then conclude.

- A **narrative** text may have an introduction, a development, a crisis and a resolution.

Page 8.

What makes a good structure?

- The points are **well organised** – in time order (e.g. for instructions) or with the main points first.

- A new **paragraph** is used for each new point or topic.

- Paragraphs may begin with **the main point**, or a general point, and continue with the detail.

- **Connectives** show how the ideas are linked, and where the ideas are going, e.g. *in addition* or *next*.

From start to finish

Structure also refers to the way in which a text begins and ends:

- The **beginning** may introduce a topic, or draw the reader in with some powerful language or ideas.

- The **end** may sum up the passage (a conclusion), or have a surprising twist, or neatly refer back to the beginning in some way.

Top Tip!

If you are commenting on the **structure** of a text, ask yourself what type of text it is. The way it is structured needs to suit the **purpose** of the text.

Spot Check

1 How do connectives help the structure of a passage?
2 When would you expect to find a new paragraph in a text?
3 Name two different ways in which a passage could end.

Look again at this extract from a recipe.

Give two ways in which the writer has made the sequence of steps clear.

1 Chop up a red cabbage and slice it thinly. Next, heat a saucepan of clean water until it boils.

2 Carefully add the cabbage to the boiling water. Then take the pan off the heat. Leave it to cool.

Top Tip!

Try to use key words from the question in your answer. This will keep your answer really focused.

Answer

1 The writer has put numbers against each step.

2 He or she has used words like 'next' and 'then' which shows clearly the order that you do things.

Comment

This answer is simple but gains full marks. It answers the precise question. Two methods have been listed and there are quotes from the text to back up the second point.

The student uses the word 'clearly' in the answer, which shows she or he is following the question and that the answer is relevant. It's a good ploy to use!

Did You Know?

In his novel *The French Lieutenant's Woman* (1969), the author John Fowles gives the reader a choice of two endings – a happy one or a sad one.

Reading texts that discuss and review

DISCUSSION TEXTS

Look out for these key features:

Purpose and audience

- **Discussion** texts include newspaper articles on important issues and student essays.

- Their **purpose** is to analyse an issue, exploring different points of view.

- They differ from argument texts because they present a **balanced view**.

Structure

- An **introduction** states the issue to be discussed.

- Each **view**, or point, is explored in turn.

- **Connectives** help the reader through the text, e.g. *however* or *another point is …*

- A **conclusion** may summarise the arguments or give a personal view.

Language

- **Present tense** and **3rd person** (*he, she, it*), e.g. *Some evidence suggests …*

- **Formal** language and tone – the arguments are presented fairly.

Top Tip!

Most discussion texts are serious – look out for **formal** language. Most reviews are lighter in tone – look out for **informal** language.

REVIEWS

Look out for these key features:

Purpose and audience

- A **review** is a way of **giving an opinion** in detail about a book, CD, film, etc.

- It is meant to **inform** the reader, and **persuade** them to buy/read/watch the work (or not!).

- You read reviews to find out about the work.

Structure

- It often begins with some basic **information** about the work.

- A series of **paragraphs** covers different points, e.g. a book review may cover plot, characters, setting and style.

- A **conclusion** may sum up the reviewer's opinion.

Language

- **Present tense** with **3rd person** when describing the work, e.g. *The film is fabulous.*

- Sentences packed with **detail**, e.g. *It mixes rip-roaring action writing with high-tech funk.*

- Often a **friendly** and **informal tone** to get on the reader's side, e.g. *What a yawn of a book.*

Note the features of this review of a computer game:

**Games
Imperial Glory
PC/Eidos £39.99**

Basic **information** listed at the start.

Step this way commander … *Imperial Glory* takes the bloodthirsty Napoleonic era (roughly) and pits the vying continental superpowers against one another in encounters reminiscent of *Rome Total War*.

Introduction draws reader in and gives a general description of the game.

Sentences packed with **detail**.

Tactics play a key role as you bid to wheel your cavalry behind your foe, take an area of high ground or match your troops against the enemy's. And there's the added bonus of naval battles, though you'll probably leave the marine war to go to the sea dogs while you concentrate on hacking down the Queen's finest with your Cossacks.

New paragraph goes into more detail about features of the game.

Friendly and informal **tone**.

IG is an accessible and satisfying strategy game on a grand scale. A valuable addition to the ranks for any PC general.

Conclusion is a short summary of writer's view.

Did You Know?

Paperback books were not produced until 1935. They were an instant success, bringing books to a much wider audience.

1 Why should discussion texts be balanced?
2 Why might you read a CD review?
3 If a review covers plot, direction, acting and special effects, what is it reviewing?

Tone

- Tone refers to the **mood** or **style** of a piece of writing, e.g. a light-hearted tone, a serious tone or an angry tone.

- The tone a writer chooses depends on the **purpose** and **audience** of the writing. For example, an advice leaflet aimed at teenagers will have a more conversational tone than a news report in a serious newspaper.

Top Tip!

To help you identify tone, imagine you are reading the piece of writing aloud. What tone of voice would you use?

Identifying tone

To identify the tone of a piece of writing, you need to look at **word choice**, **content** and **structure**, e.g:

- Slang terms give writing a more **conversational** tone, e.g. *in your face* or *street cred*.

- Writing in the 2nd person (*you*) is **more personal** than using the 3rd person (*he/she/it*).

- Exaggeration and jokes add a **humorous** tone.

- Long sentences and paragraphs often add a **more serious** tone.

Formality

Formal language gives writing a **serious** tone. It:

- follows all the rules of English grammar

- uses more difficult or technical words, e.g. *institutions* or *population*

- uses more complex sentences, e.g. *Although he became king in October, it was not until December that ...*

Informal language gives writing a **lighter** tone. It:

- includes slang or colloquialisms, e.g. *cool* or *ain't*

- includes more contractions, e.g. *isn't, can't* or *won't*

- is more personal, e.g. *You could think about ...*

- uses simpler words, including 'fillers', e.g. *well* or *yes, but ...*

I'm Not Sure that will be Possible...

No Chance!

The review on page 25 has a personal tone in places.

Identify two phrases that are personal, and say why they have been used.

Answer

1 'Step this way commander' is personal because it addresses the reader directly, asking them to be the general in the game. It grabs your attention from the start.

2 'match your troops' imagines that you are already playing this game.

Comment

This answer gets full marks. The student has chosen two good examples and shown an understanding of the purpose of the writing.

Did You Know?

Standard English is the name given to the kind of English you are taught to write in schools. Hardly anyone speaks it, though, except newsreaders on the TV or radio.

Spot Check

1 Which piece of advice has a more gentle tone:
   – It is important for everyone's health that they drink eight glasses of water each day.
   – Can you up your water intake by drinking up to eight glasses a day?
2 Arrange in order of formality:
   – It's really nice.
   – It is perfectly delightful.
   – That's wicked, man.

The test: finding information

The questions

In the test, some short questions ask you to **find information** in the extract. Often this is the first question asked about an extract.

Here are some examples (about the extract opposite):

1 How long has Ginger been sleeping rough?

2 What part of the country is Link from?

Answering the questions

- You have to **scan** the extract to look for the information you want. Sometimes you are told where to look, e.g. *In the first paragraph, find …*

- Give **only** the information you are asked for, e.g. (question 1):

  - Six or seven months ✓

  - Ginger has been sleeping rough for six or seven months. ✓

  - Ginger has been sleeping rough for six or seven months. He comes from Birmingham. ✗

- Simply copy the key word or phrase that you are asked for. Don't add extra information. You don't need to write in complete sentences.

Top Tip!

Don't spend too long on this type of question. They are worth only 1 or 2 marks.

Did You Know?

Rudyard Kipling, the author of *Jungle Book*, once painted his golf balls red so that he could play in the snow.

 **Spot Check**

Look at these statements about questions that ask you to find information. Are they true or false?

1 You don't have to write complete sentences.

2 You need to know information that isn't in the extract.

3 They are worth a lot of marks.

Read this passage about Link, a teenager who finds himself homeless in London. It describes his first night in a street doorway.

I'd just wriggled into my sleeping-bag and dropped my head on my pack when he arrived. I heard these footsteps and thought, keep going. Go past. Please go past, but he didn't. The footsteps stopped and I knew he was looking down at me. I opened my eyes. He was just a shadow framed in the doorway. "This your place?" I croaked. Stupid question. He was going to say yes even if it wasn't, right? What I should have said was piss off. I wondered how big he was.

 "No, you're right, mate." He sounded laid back, amiable. "Just shove up a bit so I can spread my roll." I obliged and he settled himself beside me, so close we were almost touching. It felt good to be with someone. Now, if anybody else turned up it wouldn't matter. There were two of us. I felt I ought to say something so I said, "Been doing this long?" hoping he wouldn't be offended.

 "Six, seven months," he said. "You?"

 "First night."

He chuckled. "I can tell. Where you from?"

 "Up north."

 "Brum, me."

 "I can tell." It was a risk, this crack about his accent, but he only chuckled again. "Name's Ginger," he said, and waited.

(From *Stone Cold*, by Robert Swindells)

1 What was Link's reaction when he heard footsteps?

2 What reason does Link give for feeling good about sharing the doorway with someone else?

1 He wanted the person to keep going.

2 If anybody else turned up, it wouldn't matter.

The test: understanding the text

The questions

Some questions ask you to 'read between the lines' of the passage. This means looking for things that aren't always stated clearly. You need to understand what the author is **suggesting**.

Here are some examples of questions like this (all relate to the passage on page 29):

1 Write down two words or phrases which show Link is unsure about the right things to say or do.

2 Give two reasons why Link may have wanted the footsteps to 'keep going'.

3 What impression do you get of Ginger? Refer to the text in your answer.

Answering the questions

• Sometimes you are simply asked to scan for the right **words or phrases**, e.g. (question 1):

  'Stupid question', 'I felt I ought to say something'

• Sometimes you need to give a **longer answer**, e.g. (question 2):

  Link may have wanted the footsteps to keep going because he was frightened of being moved on by the police. Or he may have thought he was going to be attacked.

• You may be asked to **refer to the text** in your answer. This means quoting the relevant bit and explaining what it shows, e.g. (question 3):

  Ginger seems to be very laid back. He doesn't pretend that it is his place. Instead he says, 'No, you're right, mate'. He chuckles when he's talking to Link.

> **Top Tip!**
> You have to **imagine** what Link is feeling – it isn't stated directly.

> **Top Tip!**
> If the passage is a story, try to imagine what the characters are thinking or feeling. Getting 'under their skin' will help you answer this sort of question.

Spot Check

1 What does 'reading between the lines' mean?
2 'You can give your own opinion when answering this sort of question?' True or false?

We get different impressions of Link's state of mind in this passage (see page 29).

Complete the table by writing down two more quotations from the extract and explaining what each of them suggests about Link's state of mind.

Quotation	What this suggests about Link's state of mind
"This your place?" I croaked.	He is worried that he has taken someone else's sleeping place.

Answer

Quotation	What this suggests about Link's state of mind
"This your place?" I croaked.	He is worried that he has taken someone else's sleeping place.
I wondered how big he was.	Link was anxious in case he was going to be attacked.
I felt I ought to say something.	He is nervous about leaving a silence between them.

Comment

This answer gets full marks because it gives two suitable quotations and describes what each quotation suggests about Link's state of mind. There are several other quotations that could have been used instead, e.g. *'It felt good to be with someone'* (He is relieved not to be alone.)

Did You Know?

Bruno Hauptmann kidnapped and murdered a baby, and was sent to the electric chair in 1936. What gave him away was his habit of adding extra 'e's to the end of words. He did this in his ransom note.

The questions

Some questions ask you to comment on the way a writer **organises** the text. This means thinking about how it is put together.

Here are some examples of questions like this (all relate to the passage on page 29):

1 Why does the writer use short sentences in the first paragraph and longer ones in the second paragraph?

2 Give one way in which the writer draws the reader in at the beginning.

3 How does the writer create an atmosphere of tension in the first paragraph?

Answering the questions

• Sometimes you just have to give a **reason** for something, e.g. (question 1):

> The short sentences show that Link is tense. The longer sentences in the next paragraph show he is more relaxed.

• Sometimes you need to **refer to the text**, e.g. (question 2):

> The writer says 'he arrived' in the first sentence. We are not told who 'he' is, but we want to know, so this draws us in.

• When you give a quotation, you often need to explain why you have used it. *The writer says 'he arrived' in the first sentence* is not enough on its own, because it doesn't explain the **effect** of the words quoted.

Top Tip!

If the question begins 'How does the author …?', then you are being asked to **explain** the way the author has used words or structure. Back up each point with a quotation from the passage. Make sure you **explain** why the quotation has been used.

Spot Check

1 Why are paragraphs used in a text?
2 Why is the beginning of a text particularly important?

Read the final seven lines of the passage on page 29.

"Six, seven months," he said. "You?"

"First night."

He chuckled. "I can tell. Where you from?"

"Up north."

"Brum, me."

"I can tell." It was a risk, this crack about his accent, but he only chuckled again. "Name's Ginger," he said, and waited.

Why do the paragraphs suddenly become much shorter at this point? What effect does this have?

Answer

The paragraphs become shorter because the characters are having a conversation. Each speech begins a new line.

Comment

This answer gets half marks. It explains clearly why the writer has used shorter paragraphs, but it doesn't describe the effect of this. To get full marks the student needs to add a comment like this:

It suggests they are talking quickly, in short bursts, especially the very short sentences such as 'First night'.

This includes a quotation from the extract to give an example.

Did You Know?

One short story by Franz Kafka has these famous opening lines:

As Gregor Samsa awoke one morning from uneasy dreams he found himself transformed in his bed into a gigantic insect.

The questions

Some questions ask you to comment on the writer's **use of language** – the **meaning** of certain words, or the **effect** of certain words.

Here are some examples of questions like this (all relate to the passage opposite):

1 In the first sentence, what does 'mischievous little fellow' suggest that the writer feels about frost?

2 What is the effect of describing frost patterns as 'sparkling sculptures' (paragraph 2)?

3 In the whole passage, how does the writer's choice of language make you feel that frost is something attractive?

Answering the questions

- Sometimes your answers will be quite short, e.g. (question 1):

It suggests that the writer thinks frost is fun and plays tricks on us.

- In the longer answers you need to **refer to the text**, e.g. (question 3):

The writer makes you feel frost is attractive by using the image of the artist or sculptor. In the first paragraph he 'paints intricate patterns', and in the third paragraph the patterns are described as 'delicate'. Both of the adjectives 'intricate' and 'delicate' make the patterns sound attractive.

> **Top Tip!**
>
> In your longer answers, it is often a good idea to refer to the words of the question in your answer. For example, the answer to question 3 begins
>
> *The writer makes you feel frost is attractive …*
>
> This keeps you focused on answering the question, and shows the examiner that you are answering the question!

Question

Read this newspaper article. The author explores the legend of Jack Frost and explains how frost affects the landscape.

WEATHERWATCH

Every winter a mischievous little fellow persists in painting intricate patterns on cars, windows, leaves and rocks. Legend has it that Jack Frost was the son of the Norse god of wind, Kari. Originally he was known as Jokul [icicle] Frosti [frost], which became Jack Frost when he emigrated to the UK.

Cold, clear nights with a light wind blowing and temperatures close to freezing are perfect for Jack Frost. Valleys and hollows receive more visits because cold air sinks into low-lying areas. His favourite places to create his sparkling sculptures include rocky, glass or metal surfaces because they radiate heat and cool more quickly than the air surrounding them. Car

windscreens are ideal.

Normally Jack Frost paints delicate, feather-like patterns, otherwise known as hoar frost. He interlocks ice crystals, which grow outwards from a small seed, such as a tiny lump or scratch on the surface. But if the air is moist (often foggy) and the

wind a little more breezy then Jack Frost switches to the rime frost technique. Grainy needles grow outwards, lining themselves up with the wind direction and giving structures like electricity pylons a spiky white coat.

Kate Ravilious

(Copyright Guardian Newspapers Limited 2005)

How suitable is the image of a 'spiky white coat' to describe the effect of rime frost (paragraph 3)?

Answer

The image describes how a whole structure is covered, like a coat covers a person. It is a white coat because the frost is white.

Did You Know?

The longest word in the English language is 'smiles'. (There is a mile between the first and last letter!)

Comment

This answer gets half marks. It explains two features that make the image of the coat fit the description of rime frost, but it doesn't say **how suitable** this image is, e.g.

This makes the image a very suitable one.

The student could also have referred to the 'spiky' frost resembling the material on a coat.

The test: explaining purpose and effect

The questions

Some questions ask you to comment on the **purpose** or **point of view** of the writer. They may also ask you to explain the **effect** of the text.

Here are some examples of questions like this (all relate to the passage on page 35):

1 Suggest a reason why the author begins her explanation of frost by describing the legend of Jack Frost.

2 Does the author like frost? Explain your answer.

3 The writer talks about Jack Frost throughout the article, not frost. What effect does this have?

Answering the questions

- Sometimes your answers will be quite short, e.g. (question 1):

  The author wants to grab the reader's interest at the start with a story.

- In the longer answers you need to **refer to the text**, e.g. (question 2):

  The author seems to like frost a lot. She treats it almost as a person, calling it Jack Frost and saying that 'he' has 'favourite places to create' in. She also describes the effect of frost in a positive way, with adjectives such as 'sparkling' and 'delicate'.

In the passage on page 35 the writer sets out to entertain the reader as well as to explain what frost is.

Give **three** examples of how she entertains the reader, and support each with a quotation.

Give one example from each of these categories:
• the topics covered
• the language used
• the way frost is referred to as Jack Frost.

Answer

The author tells us about the legend of Jack Frost, which is entertaining.

She uses loads of describing words like 'sparkling'.

Frost is referred to as Jack Frost, so he's like a person. He is a 'mischievous little fellow' and he 'paints delicate feather-like patterns'.

Top Tip!

The longer questions, which carry more marks, may give a **bullet point list** of topics to include in your answer. To get top marks you need to cover all the suggestions. They can also give you a structure for your answer, if you write a short paragraph on each one.

level 5

Comment

This is a level 5 answer. It shows some understanding of the purpose of the text, and of how the writer uses different techniques to achieve her purpose. It covers all the three areas suggested in the bullet points. It gives evidence from the text to back up the views.

To raise the level, the student needs to show how the quotations create the effect, e.g.

By saying that Jack Frost 'paints delicate feather-like patterns' the author makes us see frost as an artist who deliberately creates pictures and sculptures. This is an attractive way of describing frost.

Did You Know?

There is a word for the study of bird's eggs: oology (pronounced oh-ology).

If you want to move from level 4 to level 5 you need to show these skills.
(All examples relate to the passage on page 35.)

Understand purpose

You need to think about **why** the text was written. Is it to explain, or tell a story, or persuade you to buy something? Is it a mixture of different purposes? Look at this question and possible answers:

What is the purpose of the article?

To tell you about Jack Frost.

To tell you about frost in an entertaining way.

level 5

> Higher level answers would mention explanation as well as information.

Be aware of how passages are organised

You need to think about the **structure** of the text. How are paragraphs used? Why has it begun and ended as it has? Are there any layout features such as subheadings or boxes of text? Look at this question and possible answers:

Why has the author divided her article into three paragraphs?

Paragraphs are used to show different topics.

level 4

The paragraphs are used to show different topics. The first one talks about the legend of Jack Frost. The others give different kinds of information.

level 5

> Higher level answers would point out that the second paragraph describes different places and weather conditions suitable for frost, while the third paragraph describes two different types of frost.

Top Tip!

- Read the question carefully. Answer what the question asks, not what you hope it asks!
- Make sure your quotations are **relevant** to the question asked.

Understand how writers use words to create effects

You need to think about the precise **effect** that certain **words** and phrases have. They will have been chosen deliberately by the writer – why? Look at this question and possible answers:

What is the effect of the phrase 'persists in painting intricate patterns' (lines 2–3)?

It means the frost is always painting clever patterns – you can't stop it.

level 4

'Persists' makes it sound as if Jack Frost will do what he wants, and you can't stop him.

level 5

Higher level answers will comment on 'intricate patterns' as well, and on the repeated 'p' sound in the phrase.

Begin to 'read between the lines'

Think about what the writer is aiming to do. The text won't always make this clear. Often you have to work out **opinions** or **feelings** that aren't stated openly. Look at this question and possible answers:

How can you tell that the writer enjoys looking at the effects of frost? Refer to one piece of evidence from the text.

She says that the frost makes patterns.

level 4

She describes the frost as making 'delicate, feather-like patterns'.

level 5

Higher level answers will explain why this phrase shows that the writer enjoys frost.

Did You Know?

The dot on the letter 'i' is called a tipple.

The writing paper

The key things you need to know

- The writing test lasts 1 hour and 15 minutes. It is worth 50 marks.

- You are given a **question paper**. This contains two writing tasks.

- You are also given an **answer booklet**. This is just lined paper for you to write your answers on.

1HR15M

The writing tasks

- Section A is the longer writing task (30 marks). You have 45 minutes to answer this question.

- Section B is the shorter writing task (20 marks). You have 30 minutes to answer this question.

- Both tasks give you some **background**, and suggest the sort of things you should include in your answer.

- Each writing task will have a different **purpose** and **form**. For example, you may be telling a story, writing a persuasive letter or composing a report.

Pages 52–3 (different forms) and 62–71 (different purposes).

What you get marks for

- **Composition and effect**
  This means making your language and style interesting and varied. It also means writing to suit the audience and purpose given.

Pages 42–3, 46–9 and 52–3.

- **Sentence structure and punctuation**
  This means how well organised and varied your sentences are, and whether you have used punctuation correctly.

Pages 48–9 and 54–7.

- **Text structure and organisation**
  This means how well organised your whole text is, e.g. use of paragraphs and the order of your points.

Pages 50–1.

- **Spelling**
  This is marked only in the shorter writing task.

Pages 58–61.

Timing and planning

- Your teacher will remind you of the **time**, e.g. when you should be moving on to the shorter task.

- You should spend the first 15 minutes **planning** your longer writing task.

Top Tip!

Try hard to spell words correctly in the shorter writing task, as 4 out of the 20 marks are given for spelling. It could push you from a level 4 to a level 5.

Pages 44–5.

- You should spend the last 5 minutes **checking** what you have written – improving the spelling, punctuation and vocabulary.

Section A
Longer writing task
Building progress

As this is the **longer task**, you will be given a grid on which to plan your writing.

You work for a company that is building a new leisure centre. Your manager has sent you this memo:

Please report on progress so far. Write a detailed report explaining:
- how the different sports and leisure facilities are progressing (quality and speed)
- how well the construction workers are addressing the task
- whether you see any problems with the leisure centre at this stage.

A bit of **scene setting** to give you the background to the task and your role.

Write a report for your manager explaining what progress is being made in building the leisure centre.

30 marks

This tells you what the **task** is.

Did You Know?

A **blend** is a word made up of the shortened form of two other words, e.g. **heliport** (**heli**copter + air**port**).

Spot Check

True or false?
1 There are three writing tasks.
2 You are tested on spelling only in the shorter writing task.
3 Text structure and organisation is about your handwriting.

Ask yourself: What am I writing?

- Look at the **format** word in the question paper, e.g. Write a **letter**, an **account**, the first chapter of your **story**, a **leaflet**.

- Keep this format in mind as you plan and write. Most formats have special **rules**.

Pages 52–3.

- Now identify the **content**, or **topic**, that you have to write about, e.g. (a letter) describing your **visit**, or (a report) describing your **project**.

Ask yourself: Why am I writing?

- Work out your **purpose** in writing.

- **Stories** are easy – they should entertain.

- For non-fiction, though, you must look for the key word in the question. This might be: **inform**, **explain**, **describe**, **persuade**, **argue**, **advise**, **analyse**, **review** or **comment**. Understanding the purpose of the writing will mean you approach it in the right way.

Pages 66–71.

Top Tip!

Always keep **purpose**, **audience** and **role** in mind while you are planning and writing your answers. You need to keep a consistent 'viewpoint' to get a level 5.

Ask yourself: Who am I writing for?

- Keep your **audience** in mind when you plan and write. You have to adjust what you are writing to suit what they want to read.

- The audience is not the examiners, but the **person** (or people) indicated **in the question**, e.g. your fellow classmates, the head teacher, the prime minister, the manager of a factory.

Ask yourself: What is my role?

You will often be told to imagine you are a **particular person**, e.g. a resident of a certain place, a head teacher, a newspaper reporter. This is your 'role'. **Get in role** and keep in role. This means:

- not changing your **point of view**, e.g. from student to teacher, or from 3rd person to 1st person.

- not changing the **formality** of the language, e.g. from formal to informal, unless for deliberate effect.

Pages 26–7.

- not changing the **tone**, e.g. from light-hearted to serious.

Look again at the writing task from page 41.

How does thinking about purpose, audience and role help you approach the task?

> ### Section A
> ### Longer writing task
> ### Building progress
>
> You work for a company that is building a new leisure centre. Your manager has sent you this memo:
>
> > Please report on progress so far. Write a detailed report explaining:
> > - how the different sports and leisure facilities are progressing (quality and speed)
> > - how well the construction workers are addressing the task
> > - whether you see any problems with the leisure centre at this stage.
>
> **Write a report for your manager explaining what progress is being made in building the leisure centre.**
>
> *30 marks*

This is your **role** – you work for a building company. You need to keep this role going through the writing.

This list suggests the **content** of your report. You could **organise** the report into three sections like this.

In the task, you are given:
- the **form** of the writing (a report)
- the **purpose** of the writing (to explain)
- the **audience** of the writing (your manager).

So the report should be clear, formal, logical and polite.

Did You Know?

The most common word used in conversation is 'I'.

Spot Check

Match the question with the correct purpose.

Question	Purpose
1 Give your views on …	To inform or describe
2 Tell x how to …	To persuade
3 Give an account of …	To instruct
4 Inspire your team …	To argue

Planning is important

- You must spend time planning the answers to both writing tasks.

- Planning makes you **think carefully** about the task, instead of writing the first thing that comes into your head.

- It improves the **content** of your writing. You have time to think up good ideas.

- It also improves the **structure** of your writing. You can organise it instead of just rambling on.

Planning for the longer task

- You should spend the **first 15 minutes** planning your answer. Use the planning page in the question paper. (Note: the planning page isn't marked.)

- If you fill in the planning page, you will have a basic **structure** for your writing.

Planning for the shorter task

- You are not given a planning page for the shorter writing task. However, make sure you spend at least 5 minutes **thinking and planning** before you start writing.

- You can use the question paper or some spare paper to draw up a **quick plan**.

- **Brainstorm** some key words and ideas first. Then develop these ideas and put them into a sensible order.

Top Tip!

Read carefully the **detail** given in the background to the question. It will give you lots of ideas for:
(a) what to write about
(b) how to structure your answer.

Pages 64–71 (planning tools).

Spot Check

True or false?
1 You are given a planning page for both writing tasks.
2 You should spend at least 5 minutes planning for the shorter writing task.
3 Planning helps you organise your writing more effectively.

This is a planning page for the question:

Write the beginning of a short story about someone who has been left on their own.

You may wish to use this page to plan your work.
(This page will not be marked.)

Notes for description of character
- astronaut – unnamed (1st person)
- normally cool and calm
- dressed in full gear, heavy helmet, etc.

Notes for description of setting
- space station
- set in future, 2500
- huge area, lots of levels
- vast banks of computers
- completely empty – very eerie
- station circling a new, black planet

Notes on what happens in the story
- I wake up, after a year's 'frozen' sleep
- all companions gone – feelings of being alone
- explore space station, signs that it was left in a hurry – why?
- computer tells me we're being sucked into dark planet

This planning page helps you gather ideas for a **story**.

The notes are **short** and **simple**.

Jot ideas in the boxes as they occur to you.

Only this panel can be used to **structure** the story.

Did You Know?

Charles Dickens was involved in one of the first train crashes in history, when his train plunged over a bridge in 1864. Many people died, and the author never recovered from the experience.

A **wide vocabulary** helps your writing in many ways:

It makes it more interesting

* Adjectives and adverbs improve your descriptions, e.g.
  He lay the axe on the ground. ✗
  He lay his battered axe wearily on the ground. ✓

* Longer, more difficult words are often impressive, e.g.
  an atrocious attack, un unacceptable request.

It makes it more precise

* Try to avoid nouns and verbs that are very general, e.g.
  She ran to the shops. ✗
  She jogged all the way to the newsagent's on the corner. ✓

* The exact noun or verb you use creates a particular effect:
  The cat lounged in the summer house.
  The cat whimpered in the shed.

It makes it more suitable

Choose words to suit the purpose and audience of your writing:

* more **formal** words for a discussion piece, e.g. *locate, conclusion*

* some **informal** words for a teenage audience, e.g. *cool, kids*

* **emotive** words in persuasive writing, e.g. *broken-hearted, abandoned*

* **technical** words in information writing, e.g. *species, habitat*

Top Tip!

When you are checking through your work, don't be afraid to cross words out and replace them with better ones. You will get marks for using a higher level word, even if it is spelt incorrectly.

Spot Check

1 Think of four alternatives for the word 'bad'.
2 Rank them in order of 'badness' (the worst at the end).
3 Which of these words would you **not** use in a formal discussion?
wonderful, spectacular, fab, delightful, stimulating

This is a level 5 student's review.

Read the examiner's comments on the vocabulary used.

level
5

Philip Pullman has written a great end to 'His Dark Materials' trilogy – 'The Amber Spyglass', which is just as well written as 'Northern Lights' and 'The Subtle Knife' - the first two titles in the trilogy. The conflict in the other books gets bigger and bigger and seems to involve the whole universe.

Will and Lyra have become separated, they are being hunted down by terrible powers, and they are trying to find each other and their friends. Will and Lyra are the two main characters. They are beautifully drawn characters, and I nearly cried at the end.

It's a great adventure story, and goes at a great pace, with lots of twists and turns. All the characters from the rest of the trilogy are involved such as Lord Asriel, Mrs Coulter, and my favourite Iorek Byrnison the king of the armoured bears. Will and Lyra are the most important characters, however, as I've said.

The language of the book is difficult at times, but it's still a fantastic story which beats 'Harry Potter' and even 'Lord of The Rings'.

Comment

Some **precise** and **interesting** words and phrases used, such as *terrible powers*, *beautifully drawn* and *twists and turns*. Some **technical terms** appropriate for a review used (*pace*, *trilogy*, *characters*). However, the adjectives often **lack variety and power**, such as *great* and *bigger*.

Did You Know?

The English word with the largest number of meanings is 'set'. One English dictionary lists 58 uses of 'set' as a noun and 126 uses as a verb.

Making your sentences interesting

Vary the type of your sentences

- Most sentences are **statements**, e.g. *The CD cost £14.99.*

- You can add **variety** by including other types of sentence:
  - **questions**, e.g. *How much does this CD cost?* (Note the question mark.)
  - **exclamations**, e.g. *Only £14.99!* (Note the exclamation mark.)
  - **commands**, e.g. *Buy this CD for me!*

Vary the length of your sentences

- **Short sentences** often have only one clause, e.g.
  Tammy borrowed £5 from her brother.
  They are useful in instructions and straightforward information text.

- **Longer sentences** combine clauses with 'and' or 'but', e.g.
  Tammy borrowed £5 from her brother and didn't pay him back.
  Don't construct too many sentences like this: *... and ... and ... and then ...*

- Combine clauses in different ways to make sentences **more precise** and **more interesting**.
  - Use **connectives** such as 'although' and 'when', e.g. *Tammy borrowed £5 from her brother since she had left her purse behind.*
  - Include **relative** clauses (which ..., who ..., that ...) to add information, e.g. *Tammy borrowed £5 from her brother, who never let her forget it.*

Other kinds of variety

- **Begin** your sentences in different ways:
  He went to the arcade. He played on the games. He ... ✗
  He went to the arcade. After he'd played on the games, he ... ✓

- Expand your nouns with **noun phrases**:
  She was given an alarm clock. ✗
  She was given an alarm clock designed to leap about instead of making a sound. ✓

> **Top Tip!**
> Remember that every sentence must make sense on its own. This almost always means that every sentence has a verb.

Did You Know?
You should never write 'would of' or 'should of'. The correct form is 'would have' or 'should have', e.g. *I would have got full marks.*

Look again at the level 5 student's review from page 47. This time, concentrate on the **sentence structure**.

Philip Pullman has written a great end to 'His Dark Materials' trilogy – 'The Amber Spyglass', which is just as well written as 'Northern Lights' and 'The Subtle Knife' – the first two titles in the trilogy. The conflict in the other books gets bigger and bigger and seems to involve the whole universe.

Will and Lyra have become separated, they are being hunted down by terrible powers, and they are trying to find each other and their friends. Will and Lyra are the two main characters. They are beautifully drawn characters, and I nearly cried at the end.

It's a great adventure story, and goes at a great pace, with lots of twists and turns. All the characters from the rest of the trilogy are involved such as Lord Asriel, Mrs Coulter, and my favourite lorek Byrnison the king of the armoured bears. Will and Lyra are the most important characters, however, as I've said.

The language of the book is difficult at times, but it's still a fantastic story which beats 'Harry Potter' and even 'Lord of The Rings'.

Good points:
– includes relative clauses to add information;
– clauses have been added to make sentences longer;
– some noun phrases and connectives add interest and detail.

Could improve by:
– avoiding using too many dashes to add information;
– avoiding beginning sentences with the same words;
– combining clauses using connectives other than 'and'.

Spot Check

Combine these sentences to make them more interesting:
Kevin took the bus to town. He didn't want to miss the start of the film. He pushed through the crowds.

The key things you need to know

- A paragraph is a group of sentences on one topic. Paragraphs are used to **organise** your writing and to help the reader **follow your ideas**.

- You begin a new paragraph when you talk about a **new point**, **character**, **place** or **time**.

- You show it's a new paragraph by leaving a line space, or starting the new line slightly in from the margin.

Ordering paragraphs

- This is where **planning** is vital. Each main item in your plan will often become a separate paragraph.

Pages 44–5.

- Number the items on your plan to give you a **sensible order** for your paragraphs.

- The **first paragraph** must grab the reader's attention. (In some non-fiction texts, it may be a general introduction.)

- Your **final paragraph** must be a definite ending.

Top Tip!

When checking your work, you can use an insertion mark and write ⓝⓟ, where you want to start a new paragraph.

Signalling where you are going

- Use **topic sentences** to start each paragraph. These give the main point of the paragraph. Then develop the point by adding reasons, examples, etc.

- Show where your sentences are going by using **connectives**, e.g. *Yet ...* (= here's an opposite point), and **signposts**, e.g. *The following day ...* (= to tell you when) and *Other people disagree ...* (= to tell you who).

Spot Check

1 Give two reasons why you would start a new paragraph.
2 'You need a new paragraph every 10 or 15 lines.' True or false?
3 Explain what a topic sentence is.

This example of an advice text gains a level 5 for its organisation and structure.

level 5

How to deal with rejection

When a relationship breaks up, it can be a very painful experience, especially if it happens quickly. You can feel a shock, almost as if your friend has died.

If the relationship was a really good one, it's normal to feel grief that it's over. So don't think that it's wrong to get some of the grief out of your system by having a good cry. If the relationship is clearly over, don't waste time trying to patch it up. If you go round pleading with your ex-boyfriend/girlfriend to take you back, you're only prolonging the agony. You're more likely to turn them off than win them back.

Finally, don't worry that you'll never make another relationship. When a relationship ends, it can be difficult to think there'll be others. But there will be!

Also, one thing people do when they're rejected is to ask themselves what went wrong. Remember that relationships end for all sorts of reasons, and it's hardly ever one person's fault.

Logical point to put at the beginning. ✓

Main point given first (topic sentence), then developed. ✓

Need a new paragraph here, as it's a new point. ✗

This paragraph would be better at the end. ✗

Connectives show how the ideas are linked. ✓

Sob

Did You Know?

The Unfortunates (1969) is a novel supplied in a box. Its author, Bryan Johnson, provides the first and last chapters but presents the rest as single pages that can be read in any order.

Writing in different formats

Letters

- **Lay out** the letter properly.

- Most letters need a **formal** style, e.g. a letter of complaint, a letter to a newspaper, or to apply for a job.

- Some letters will be more **informal**, e.g. a letter to a friend or relative.

Page 53.

Pages 26–7 (formality).

Newspaper stories

- Write in a **clear but lively** style. Use **short paragraphs** and **short sentences**.

- The first paragraph often gives the main information – answering the questions 'who', 'what', 'where' and 'when'. Later paragraphs give further details.

- Include **quotes** from people involved, or comments from experts, e.g. *Ben Potts, a neighbour, said, "…"*.

- Add a snappy **headline**.

Leaflets

- **Presentation** – include bullet points and subheadings to break up the text. Leave spaces for graphics, pictures or logos.

- **Structure** – use short paragraphs and sentences. Include headings to guide the reader through the text.

- **Style** – use clear and simple language for information or advice leaflets. Include persuasive techniques if you are selling a product or an idea.

Top Tip!

When writing a leaflet, don't waste time on design. For example, draw an empty box and add a label (*picture of …*) rather than spending time drawing an actual picture.

Pages 70–1.

Reports

- Most reports are **factual** and **formal**, like a school report. They use clear and formal language, and a reasonable tone.

- **Impersonal phrases** and **passive verbs** are common, e.g. *It is preferable …* or *The product was assessed …*

- Give it a **logical structure** – an introduction, then the main points in order of importance, and a summary at the end.

Did You Know?

One of the shortest letters was written by the novelist Victor Hugo. Wanting to know how people were reacting to his latest novel, he wrote to his publishers: '?' They replied: '!'

- Remember that the audience will be **listening** to the speech, so try and imagine someone reading it aloud. Some good **sound effects** include:
  - **repetition**, e.g. *It's time to protest, and to protest with force.*
  - **alliteration**, e.g. *The proposal is dangerous and destructive.*
  - **lists of three**, e.g. *... for a better, fairer and more prosperous future.*

- Vary the length of your sentences for effect.

Pages 48–9.

Example

Note how this letter is set out.

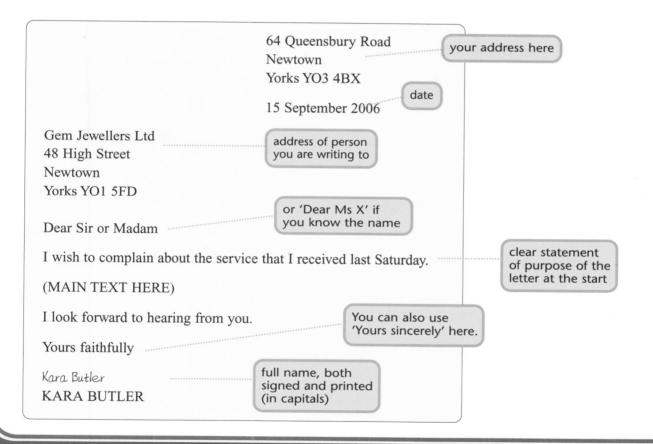

64 Queensbury Road
Newtown
Yorks YO3 4BX
— *your address here*

15 September 2006
— *date*

Gem Jewellers Ltd
48 High Street
Newtown
Yorks YO1 5FD
— *address of person you are writing to*

Dear Sir or Madam
— *or 'Dear Ms X' if you know the name*

I wish to complain about the service that I received last Saturday.
— *clear statement of purpose of the letter at the start*

(MAIN TEXT HERE)

I look forward to hearing from you.

Yours faithfully
— *You can also use 'Yours sincerely' here.*

Kara Butler
KARA BUTLER
— *full name, both signed and printed (in capitals)*

Spot Check

Which of these phrases would you include in a letter, and which would you include in a speech?

1 With reference to your advert ...
2 Are we so bad? Are we so mad?
3 Dear Sir
4 I stand before you this evening ...
5 I look forward to hearing from you

Basic rules

- Every sentence must make complete sense on its own, so it must contain a verb:
  - *Twenty minutes on the trampoline.* ✗
  - *She was on the trampoline for 20 minutes.* ✔

- Every sentence must begin with a **capital letter**.

- Capitals are also used for **proper names**, e.g. *Raj, Ipswich, Nike, Robston College.*

- Every sentence must **end** with a **full stop**, a **question mark** or an **exclamation mark**:
  - *Steve is running.* (statement)
  - *Run, Steve!* (exclamation or command)
  - *Why don't you run, Steve?* (question)

Punctuation for adding text

- A **dash** adds a short bit of information, e.g.
  I put it here – no, here.
  Do not overuse dashes.

- A **colon** introduces a list, e.g.
  These are our demands: £10,000 in cash, a getaway car …

- You can **mark off extra information** by using dashes, brackets or commas:
  The culprit – or so it appeared – had slipped away.
  The culprit (or so it appeared) had slipped away.

Pages 56–7.

Apostrophes

- An apostrophe is used where words have been **shortened**, e.g. *haven't* (have not), *I'm* (I am), *he's* (he is), *let's* (let us), *they're* (they are). Note that the apostrophe is put where the missing letter should be.

- Apostrophes also tell you who **owns something**:
  - for **singular**, add apostrophe + **s**, e.g. *Brett's car, United's win*
  - for **plural**, add the apostrophe after the **s**, e.g. *a friends' gathering*

- Do not confuse apostrophes with speech marks.

Top Tip!

Remember that 'its' is used to show ownership (like 'his' and 'hers'), e.g. *She pulled its tail.* 'It's' stands for 'it is', e.g. *It's raining.*

Example

This level 4 writing has some correct punctuation, but needs to improve to get a level 5.

level
4

Have you heard people say that soaps are just like real life They are'nt nearly as realistic as real life, for several reasons – first of all, people die (or disappear) far more often in soaps. This is because of the actor's desire to leave the series after a period. If a key figure wants to leave, the producer has only two option's. One is to kill him off and the other is divorce. Also theres always something happening in characters lives in soaps in real life its actually quite boring.

> Question mark missing.

> You need to start a new sentence here.

> Incorrect use of apostrophe.

Did You Know?

The wrong use of an apostrophe in words that are just plurals is known as the 'greengrocer's apostrophe'. This is because it is so common to see signs like this at greengrocers' stalls.

Apple's half price

Spot Check

1 When do you need to use a capital letter?
2 Add the punctuation:
   graemes mobile rang it was paula calling from oxford
3 Correct the punctuation:
   'Its endless is'nt it!' she said – looking at: the minute's go by.

What is a comma?

The comma is a very useful and common punctuation mark. It is used in many different ways to **separate words**, **phrases and clauses** in a sentence. Using the comma well in your writing shows:
– that you can organise your sentences, so that their meaning is clear.
– that you can use punctuation accurately.

Separating words and phrases

- The comma must be used to **separate items in a list**:
  Please put all clothes, books, swimming and sporting equipment, mobile phones and other personal belongings in the lockers provided.
  Note that the final item before 'and' (*mobile phones*) does not need a comma after it.

- The comma is used to **separate a phrase** that gives extra information about something:
  The third from the right, the woman in the hat, is the winner!

Separating the main parts of a sentence

- The comma is used to **separate the main parts of a sentence**:
  Although Keith ran as fast as he could, he still came last.
  Rebecca agreed to look after the dog, which was the worst decision she had ever made.

Avoiding the comma

- Think about what really links the clauses of a sentence. Often using a comma is not the best form of punctuation:
  To display web pages you need software called a browser, this converts the coded pages into a form that you can read on the computer. ✗
  Here the second clause is just 'tagged on'. You should use a **colon** instead of a comma, or start a new sentence:
  To display web pages you need software called a browser. This converts the coded pages into a form that you can read on the computer. ✓

Top Tip!
Do not overuse commas. Think about using other punctuation marks as well.

Look at how one student has used commas in this piece of writing.

level
5

Lots of girls want to look like the celebrities they see on TV, but celebrities have to look amazing, it's what they are paid to do. Unlike ordinary people, they have the time and money to achieve that perfect look. Most of the girls you see around town, would look just as fantastic if they had personal trainers, beauticians, stylists and dieticians at their fingertips. Remember too that celebrities use top photographers, who are trained to get the best out of their subject. So don't judge your looks against photographs of top models: it simply isn't a fair comparison.

Colon or dash would be better than a comma here. ✗

No comma needed here. ✗

Comma separates items in a list. ✓

Comma used to separate clauses. ✓

Colon better than a comma here. ✓

Comment

This is a level 5 piece of writing. Commas are mostly used accurately and effectively. They show the structure of the sentences clearly. Other punctuation is sometimes used instead of commas where necessary.

Did You Know?

The final chapter of James Joyce's novel *Ulysses* consists of eight enormous sentences. It goes on for over 60 pages and has no punctuation.

Spot Check

Add commas to these sentences:
1 He used the colours red white yellow and blue.
2 Lucy the youngest of the children is really the most important character.
3 Stuart was replaced at half-time which was the final straw.

Spelling: endings and beginnings

Plurals

Add **-s** to make the plural of a word, e.g. *house → houses, pool → pools*.

Exceptions:

- Words ending in **-ss, -sh, -ch, -x**: you add **-es**, e.g. *glasses, matches, foxes.*

- Words ending in consonant + **y**: you change **-y** to **-ies**, e.g. *lady → ladies, try → tries.*

- Words ending in **-f**: you usually change **-f** to **-ves**, e.g. *loaf → loaves, leaf → leaves.*

- Some words don't follow these rules, e.g. *children, women, mice, sheep.*

Verbs

Add **-ing** or **-ed** to make different parts of the verb, e.g. *form → forming, formed; watch → watching, watched.*

Exceptions:

- Short verbs ending in vowel + consonant: you double the consonant, e.g. *drop → dropping, dropped; fit → fitting, fitted.*

- Verbs ending in **-e**: you drop the **-e**, e.g. *decide → deciding, decided; state → stating, stated.*

- Many common verbs have different forms in the past tense, e.g. *fight → fought, begin → began, meet → met.*

Prefixes and suffixes

- **Prefixes** are letters added at the **start** of a word to change its meaning:

  - **in-, un-, im-, ir-, mis-** and **dis-** often form opposites, e.g. *invisible, unfair, impossible, mistrust.*
  - **pre-** and **fore-** mean 'in front' or 'before', e.g. *prefer, foreground.*

- Prefixes do not change the spelling of the original word.

- **Suffixes** are letters added at the **end** of a word to change its meaning:

  - **-able, -ible** and **-uble** mean that something is possible, e.g. *legible, soluble.*
  - **-ful** means 'full of', e.g. *careful, peaceful.* (Note: not **-full**.)

- You drop a final **-e** before a suffix that begins with a vowel, e.g. *forgive + -able = forgivable*

Top Tip!

Your spelling is marked only in the shorter writing task. Don't relax, though – a fifth of the marks in that test go on spelling!

Look at this extract from a level 4 answer to a shorter writing task.

> I don't beleive in horroscopes at all. No one knowes about the future but Allah. Sometimes they come true but I think that it's considence. On Wendnesday the horoscope said: "Something bad will happen today". I worryed all day, and then I cought a cold. But surley everyday there's something bad that happens!

level
4

The student checked her spelling at the end of the test and made these corrections, which took her answer up to a level 5.

> I don't believe in horoscopes at all. No one knows about the future but Allah. Sometimes they come true but I think that it's coincidence. On Wednesday the horoscope said: "Something bad will happen today". I worried all day, and then I caught a cold. But surely every day there's something bad that happens!

level
5

Did You Know?

'Dreamt' is the only English word ending in 'mt'.

Spot Check

1 Which are the incorrect plurals?
churches, potatoes, flys, wolves, gasses

2 Add **-ing** and **-ed** to these verbs:
skate, skid, respect

3 Give the past tense of these verbs:
find, steal, travel, buy

Use a dictionary

- The best way to master spelling is to look words up in a **dictionary** while you are writing.

- Do *not* use spell checker programs. They make you a lazy speller.

- Note: you are not allowed to use a dictionary in the tests.

Collins
Easy Learning
**English
Dictionary**

The easiest way to succeed in English

List your spelling bugs

- **Make a list** of words you regularly misspell. Make a bookmark out of it. Learn them.

- **Learn** these commonly misspelt words:
  all right
  believe
  character
  clothes
  coming
  definite
  friend
  quiet
  receive
  separate

Sob

friend
A freind in need …

Top Tip!

You will get credit for using a complicated word in your test, even if you misspell it.

Beware of homophones

- Some common words **sound the same** but are spelt differently. Learn these and look out for others:

  – *their* (belonging to them), *they're* (= they are), *there* (where)

  – *wear* (clothes), *we're* (= we are), *where* (here), *were* (past tense of are)

  – *are* (present tense of were), *our* (belonging to us)

  – *to* (go to bed), *too* (much), *two* (2)

  – *whose* (belonging to someone), *who's* (= who is)

whose
Who's clothes are these?

Other spelling tips

- Learn a few **spelling rules**.

Pages 58–9.

- Use **memory joggers**, e.g. Remember there is *iron* in the envi**ron**ment, a *rat* in sepa**rat**e, **finite** in de**finite** and a **cog** in re**cog**nise.

- **Say the word** in your mind as it is spelt, e.g. *Feb**ru**ary, Wed**nes**day*.

- Break words into smaller chunks, e.g. *ex-treme-ly, re-le-vant*.

A student has checked this paragraph and corrected the spelling in places. Read the paragraph and the examiner's comment.

> Bad behaveour basicly doesn't start in the
> classroom, it starts in sociatey. You're not going to be
> naughty
> ~~naugthy~~) in school for no reason. Exclusion isn't a
> good idea – it's just like giving them a holiday. They
> should keep them in school longer really, at
> weekends. If the kid has broken the law then the
> ought
> police ~~aught~~ to definately be involved, but if no
> committed
> crime is ~~commited~~ bad behaveour is just a matter
> for the school.

Comment

Spelling of simple words is correct. Some common longer words are accurately spelt, e.g. *involved*, *committed*. But some words are misspelt – *basicly* (basically), *behaveour* (behaviour), *sociatey* (society), *definately* (definitely) – so 2 out of 4 marks are awarded.

Did You Know?

The first printers added letters to the ends of words to straighten the right-hand edge of their texts. Spelling wasn't so important in the Middle Ages!

Spot Check

1 Which of these words are spelt incorrectly?
queitly, dissappoint, believe, friend, wierd, necessary, ocasion
2 What is the difference between *their* and *there*?
3 Give a memory jogger that helps you spell.

Planning and structure

- If you are given a story to write, it will probably be for the longer writing task. Use the **planning grid** on the question paper.

Pages 44–5.

- You also need to plan the **structure** of your story carefully:

  - Give your story a **beginning** (when you introduce the plot/setting/characters), a **middle** (when you develop plot and character) and an **ending** (when things are sorted out, or you keep the reader guessing with a cliffhanger).

  - If you want a **fast moving** story, make it exciting and full of tension.

  - If you want a **slow moving** story, focus more on character, feelings and description.

Top Tip!

Before you begin writing, think about how you are going to end your story. A cliffhanger ending is deliberate – it isn't just an ending that tails off.

Characters

- Your characters need to be **believable** and **interesting**. Don't include more than two or three.

- Describe characters by how they **look**, what they **say** and what they **do**. Often their feelings are better **implied** than stated directly:
  The children felt very cold. ✗
  The children huddled together, their teeth chattering. ✔

- Get **under the skin** of the main character and write from their point of view.

- Keep your **viewpoint consistent**. If you begin writing as the main character (using 'I'), stick to it.

Shiver

Speech

- Speech adds variety to your story. It also **develops the characters and the plot** and brings both to life.

- Make speech **realistic**. People speak in short sentences and use slang. Think how *you* would speak in that situation.

- Follow the rules for **punctuating** speech, and other guidelines.

Page 63.

Language

- Make your sentences **interesting**. Think carefully about the words that you use. In particular:

  – Use **adjectives** and **adverbs** to give descriptive detail, especially to create the setting.

  – Use powerful **nouns** and **verbs** for effect.

  – Include some **imagery**.

  – **Vary** the length and type of your sentences.

Page 18 (imagery) and pages 48–9 (variety).

Example

Follow these guidelines when writing dialogue.

> Begin a new paragraph each time the speaker changes.

> Note how Keith's speech is informal, but Jim's is formal.

The policeman grabbed Keith by the collar. "Not so fast, lad," he whispered in his ear.

"Ow, leggo!" yelled Keith. "I ain't done nothin'."

Jim heard the commotion and turned back. "It's all right, officer," he called reassuringly. "I can explain everything."

> Put speech marks around the words that are spoken.

> Vary your words for 'said'.

Did You Know?

The initials of J R R Tolkien, the author of *Lord of the Rings*, stand for John Ronald Reuel.

Spot Check

1 What is the basic structure for a story?
2 'The more characters the better.' True or false?
3 Give two rules to follow when including dialogue.

The key things you need to know

- You may be asked to describe an **event**, **place** or **person**. Your aim is to tell the readers about it in an interesting and entertaining way.

- Descriptions mean giving more than the facts. You have to **bring the event, person or place to life** by using language effectively.

Planning and structure

- A **spider diagram** is good for planning description. Brainstorm **different ideas** on the subject. Then decide on the **order**.

- Start with the main idea in the middle and branch out like this:

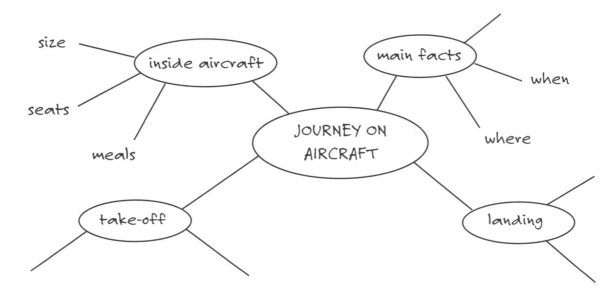

Descriptive language

- Use the **senses**. Describe what you see, smell, hear, touch, taste and feel, e.g.
  I jumped as the elephant lifted its trunk and bellowed.

- Use **powerful words** instead of dull words, e.g.
  The town ~~was full of~~ rang with the cries of street sellers.

- Include some special **imagery** if you can, e.g.
  His eyebrows scuttled like spiders across his brow.

- Go into **detail**. Precise description is more powerful than general comments, e.g.
  I put on my ~~hat~~ thick green bobble hat and opened the door.

- **Vary** the length and type of your sentences.

Top Tip!

The description does *not* have to be true, but it has to be believable.

Page 18.

Pages 48–9.

This is the beginning of a description of 'a memorable journey'. Read the comments on the **good points**, and on the **things that would improve the writing**.

My first trip on an aeroplane was when I was about six. We were going on holiday to Spain, just like millions of other people, but it was a new experience for me.

Everything was strange, even before we got on the aircraft I could see vast halls full of people. Our suitcases disappeared behind some flaps, like they were being eaten by a mechanical monster. There were lots of officials in uniform who always knew where they were going.

Structure is careful and clear. 1st paragraph gives the background. ✓

Language could be more lively and interesting, e.g. 'Our destination was …' ✗

Description in the 2nd paragraph conveys writer's feeling of being overwhelmed. Good simile of monster. ✓

Could replace some dull words, e.g. 'got on' with 'boarded', 'could see' with 'was transfixed by'. 'Everything was strange' would make a powerful 1st sentence on its own. ✗

Did You Know?

A cliché is a phrase that has been over-used, which makes it dull and lifeless. Examples are 'take the bull by the horns' and 'a blessing in disguise'.

Spot Check

1 Give one reason why a spider diagram is useful for planning descriptions.
2 Why are adjectives useful in descriptive writing?
3 What is imagery?

Writing to inform and explain

Structure and planning

- Spider diagrams are useful planning tools when writing **information**.

Page 64.

- A step-by-step planning tool works well when writing **explanation** texts e.g.

- Use **paragraphs** to organise your writing – one paragraph for each bubble on the diagram.

- Use **connectives** to guide the reader through the text and link the paragraphs, e.g. *first, then, in addition, for example, because, as a result, when, therefore.*

- Begin with a clear **introduction**.

Content and language

- Information and explanation texts are mainly **facts**. They need to be **clear**. Avoid persuasive or very descriptive language.

- Use **formal** English, in the **3rd person** (unless the facts are about you):
  I hang out in a youth club, but there's another one too. ✗
  Teenagers have the choice of two youth clubs. ✓

Pages 42 and 46.

Top Tip!

Remember your **audience** when writing. Children will need a different approach to (say) parents or older people.

- Begin each paragraph with a **general statement** (topic sentence), then continue with further **detail** or **examples**, e.g.
  Animals can do some extraordinary things. Pumas, for example, can jump up to 20 metres.

Pages 50–1.

This is an extract from an information sheet that a student wrote about their own house, for a 'time capsule'. Read the comments on the good points, and on the things that would improve the writing.

It was built in the 1890s from Cotswold stone. The house is attached to both its neighbours, forming a terrace of three. There is plenty of space for a family of five, it is spread over four floors. The ground floor consists of a small entrance hall which leads to a double-sized living room with an open fire, piano and hi-fi.

At one end (of the ground floor) is a large kitchen extension. At the other is a south-facing conservatory with a sofa and TV. There is a downstairs toilet.

On the first floor is a large single bedroom and a bathroom with a walk-in shower ...

Better to begin with the subject: 'The house, built in the 1890s, ...' ✗

Better to begin a new paragraph with 'The ground floor', as it's a new topic. ✗

Very factual, lots of nouns – not trying to 'sell' house to a buyer. ✓

Needs some connectives to guide reader, e.g. 'also', 'in addition'. ✗

All formal and consistently in the 3rd person. ✓

New topic, so new paragraph. ✓

Did You Know?

English borrows from many other languages, e.g. *hamburger* (German), *kayak* (Eskimo) and *shampoo* (Hindi).

Spot Check

1 'The main aim of an information text is to entertain the reader.' True or false?

2 Why is a step-by-step planning tool useful for explanation texts?

3 Give three connectives that you might use in an information or explanation text.

Structure and planning

- A spider diagram is a useful planning tool for a **review**. Give each feature of the book, film, etc. a different bubble, e.g.
  - for a **book**: plot, characters, language, themes
  - for a **film**: plot, acting, special effects, direction

Page 64.

- Begin with **information** about the product, then **one paragraph per feature**, then **sum up** your view.

- Use the planning tool on the right for a balanced **discussion**.

- Use **connectives** to guide the reader through the discussion, e.g. *therefore, in addition, on the other hand, however*.

- Make it clear **who holds what views**, e.g. *Other people say …, Opponents argue …*

1 Introduction to issue: ————————	
2 Points for _____ _____	3 Points against _____ _____
4 Conclusion – summing up (include your view) _____	

Language and style

- In **discussion** texts:

  - use **formal** language, e.g. *A view shared by many is that …*

  - give **examples** and **quote** people's views, e.g.
    Sandra, for example, says, 'Smokers should pay for their own hospital bills.' (direct speech)
    Sandra believes that smokers should pay for their own hospital bills. (indirect speech)

  - present people's views **fairly** – put your own view in the **conclusion**.

- In **reviews**:

  - your style can be more **lively and informal**, e.g. *Flip to the end and you'll get a shock.*

  - cover both the **good and bad points** of the product.

  - include your **own view** throughout, e.g. *I felt that …*

  - write in the **present tense**, e.g. *The special effects are amazing, the characters fail to convince.*

Top Tip!

In a discussion piece, it is OK to make up the evidence (people's views), as long as it is realistic.

SMOKERS SHOULD PAY FOR THEIR OWN HOSPITAL BILLS.

Pages 47 and 49 (reviews).

This is the start of a discussion which analyses the results of a survey on attitudes to single-sex schools. Read the comments on the good points, and on the things that would improve the writing.

level
4

Both parents and students are deeply divided on the issue, as this survey shows.

It's mostly girls who say 'yes' to single-sex schools, like Louise, who says 'They allow students to learn, without getting distracted by boys'. And I think you can 'be yourself' more at an all-girls school. But some boys like them too. For example, Greg says you can see girls plenty after school.

Others, like Yajnah, are anti. They think ...

Structure:

– first paragraph is introduction
– one paragraph for each set of views
– connectives used to guide reader, e.g. 'but', 'for example' ✓

– introduction needs to say what the issue is: single-sex schools ✗

Language/style:

– mostly formal language (but see below)
– mostly a balanced approach (but see below)
– refers to people's views in detail ✓

– some slips, e.g. 'are anti'
– the writer includes own view once ✗

Did You Know?

When *Coronation Street* first hit the TV screens in 1960, the *Daily Mirror* reviewer said, 'I find it hard to believe that viewers will want to put up with a continuous slice of domestic drudgery two evenings a week.' How wrong he was!

 **Spot Check**

1 Which is usually written in more formal language, a discussion or a review?
2 'You shouldn't include your own opinion in a review.' True or false?
3 Give two connectives that could be useful in a discussion.

Writing to persuade, argue, advise

Structure and planning

- When planning an argument, brainstorm a **series of points**, then put them in a **logical order**. This is a useful planning tool:

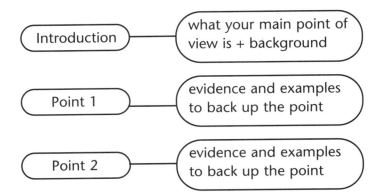

- Introduction — what your main point of view is + background
- Point 1 — evidence and examples to back up the point
- Point 2 — evidence and examples to back up the point

- Give each point a **new paragraph**.

- Begin with an **introduction** and end with a powerful **conclusion**.

- **Connectives** are important to join up your ideas, e.g. *therefore, because, firstly*.

> **Top Tip!**
> You can make up quotations from 'experts' to back up your arguments.

Language and style

- Think about the purpose and audience of the task. If you want to sound **reasonable**, use **formal language** and avoid exaggerating.

- Think of your **opponent's arguments** and try to counter them.

- Include some **rhetorical techniques**, e.g.
  - **emotive words**: *starving* (not *hungry*), *children* (not *people*)
  - **repetition**: *it isn't fair and it isn't just*
  - **alliteration**: *a **pr**essing **pr**oblem*
  - **rhetorical questions** (where the answer is obvious): *Are we to take this seriously?*
  - **personal pronouns**: *we* includes the audience, *you* addresses the audience directly

- For **more persuasive** writing, such as a speech encouraging a sports team, include more rhetorical techniques!

- When **writing to advise**, use softer language and a friendly informal tone. Include words like *should, could, may* and *perhaps*.

Page 51 (advice texts).

Look at this level 4 argument. The version below is much more persuasive (level 5).

level
4

> I think that footballers are paid the right amount of money for what they do. They are very skilful and strong and work very hard. It's a hard game so they can't play for years and years so they have to make a lot of money quickly. They give a lot of people a lot of pleasure watching them.

level
5

> Footballers are definitely paid the right amount of money for what they do. You have to admit that at the top level they are skilful and strong athletes who work very hard.
>
> Football is a tough contact sport so players have to make a lot of money quickly. They have to retire early, so what are they going to live on then?
>
> Footballers also give a huge amount of pleasure to millions of spectators.

stronger opening ('definitely')

direct address ('you')

new point, so new paragraph

rhetorical question

more powerful language

Did You Know?

Many politicians have professional speech-writers to write their speeches for them.

Spot Check

1 How do paragraphs help you structure an argument?
2 Give two rhetorical techniques.
3 Which of these adjectives would you avoid in persuasive writing?
fantastic, wonderful, amazing, good, excellent

Follow these guidelines to improve your writing from level 4 to level 5.

Structure and organisation

- **Organise** your writing in a clear way. Include an introduction and a conclusion. Make sure any story has a beginning, a middle and an end.

- Use **paragraphs** – a new paragraph for each point, or for a change of scene, character, etc.

- Include a few **connectives** (link words) to link the ideas in your sentences.

Content

- In **stories**, make your characters interesting. Try to show what they are feeling. Include some conversation to help you do this.

- In **non-fiction**, think of your main points before you start writing.

- Develop some of your ideas, e.g. by giving examples or evidence.

Language and style

- Think about the **individual words** you use. Can you make any more interesting or effective?

- Keep the **purpose** and **viewpoint** of your writing consistent: if you are writing 'in role', keep to that role.

- Try to include some **stylistic effects**, e.g. rhetorical techniques in persuasive writing.

Top Tip!

Give yourself enough checking time – this is where you can pick up those extra marks.

Punctuation, grammar and spelling

- Use **punctuation** accurately to structure your sentences and make the meaning clear.

- Don't make any basic **grammatical** errors.

- Make sure you **spell** all simple words correctly.

Remember to practise spelling!

Example

This is the start of a level 4 piece of writing. The task is to advise students on how to do their homework.

> You should follow this advice ...
>
> Try to follow a routine, like studying when you get home from school Routines are helpfull. so is taking a few breaks, don't works for hours on end please! And if you don't want to be disterbed don't do you're homework in the siting room with the telly on it will disterb you. I do this lot's and it doesn't work.

level 4

The improvements made here give it a level 5.
(Note: there are still some spelling errors, underlined in red.)

level 5

> <u>How to study</u>
>
> Do you want to improve your study skills? Then simply follow this advice ...
>
> • <u>Try to follow a routine</u>. Routines help you orginise your time. If you get into the habit of doing your homework when you get home from school, it will help.
>
> • <u>Don't work non-stop</u>. Regular breaks actually help you cos you return to work refreshed. You will get bored and fed up if you do your homework for hours on end.
>
> • <u>Don't get distracted.</u> A noisy place is a disaster if you want to do good homework effectiveley so avoid doing it on the bus, or in the television room with your mobile switched on. The interuptions will seriously distract you from doing any proper work.

Includes a title and a more effective introduction.

Each point has its own paragraph (bullet point).

Each point is developed a bit more, e.g. by giving a reason or example.

Audience and purpose is kept in mind throughout – no reference to the writer's own experience.

Language is a bit more interesting, e.g. 'distracted'.

Spelling and punctuation is more accurate (though not completely!).

Did You Know?

You can visit Collins Word Exchange to look up any English word in the dictionary, build your own dictionary, join forums to discuss word uses, and test your English skills by playing games:
www.collins.co.uk/wordexchange/

The key things you need to know

- The Shakespeare test lasts 45 minutes. It is worth 18 marks.

- You are given a **question paper**, which contains **one** question. The question focuses on extracts from the set scenes that you have been studying in class.

- You are also given an **answer booklet**. This is simply lined paper for you to write your answer on.

Top Tip!
You are not given marks for spelling or grammar. However, the examiners need to understand your ideas, so try to express yourself clearly.

You have to ...

- Answer the precise question given, which will ask you to write about the **scenes** you have been studying.

- Base your answer on the **extracts** given, though knowledge of the rest of the play and of Shakespeare's world will be useful.

Pages 76–7.

- Show that you really understand the extracts, by making **points** about them and backing up your points with **quotations**.

Pages 82–3.

What you are asked about

You will be asked a question about **one** of these four aspects of the play:

- **Character** – what the main characters do and why they behave as they do.

Pages 84–5.

- **Themes** – the particular ideas (such as love or revenge) that the play explores.

Pages 86–7.

- **Language** – what the characters say, how they say it and the effect that this has on the audience.

Pages 78–9, and 88–9.

- **Performance** – how the scenes would have been performed, and how you might put them on if you were the director.

Pages 90–1.

Timing and planning

- You should spend the first **10 minutes planning** your answer.

Pages 80–1.

- You should spend the last **5 minutes checking** what you have written.

- Your teacher will remind you of the time, e.g. halfway through the test and 5 minutes before the end.

Much Ado About Nothing

Act 1 Scene 1, lines 119 to 182
Act 2 Scene 3, lines 181 to 213

What do you learn about Benedick's attitudes to love and marriage in these extracts?

Support your ideas by referring to both of the extracts which are printed on the following pages.

18 marks

The **play** you have been studying. You will be given the question paper that relates to your play only.

The **extracts** that you have to refer to in your answer. The extracts are printed in full in the question paper.

The **question** that you have to answer.

Two reminders:
– Refer to **both** of the extracts in your answer.
– **Quote** from the extracts.

Did You Know?

There have been over 400 films made of Shakespeare's plays.

**pot Check**

True or false?
1 You are tested on your historical knowledge about Shakespeare's life and times.
2 You have to refer to all the set scenes in your answer.
3 You should spend 10 minutes planning your answer.

Shakespeare's plays

Shakespeare wrote different kinds of plays

- **Tragedies** are serious and end with the main character's death. They explore power, jealousy, ambition and love. Example: *Romeo and Juliet*.

- **Comedies** are light-hearted and have a happy ending. They explore the relationships of men and women in love, and include misunderstandings and disguise. Example: *Much Ado About Nothing*.

- **Histories** tell the story of English kings. They explore conflict, loyalty and what it means to be a king. Example: *Richard III*.

- **Romances** begin tragically and end happily. They are sometimes called 'tragicomedies'. Example: *The Tempest*.

Shakespeare's world

William Shakespeare (born 1564, died 1616) lived during the reigns of Elizabeth I and James I. The world was very different then:

- **Kings and queens** were all-powerful. People believed they were chosen by God to rule the country.

- The **upper classes** (nobles, e.g. dukes) also had a lot of power. The **lower classes** (ordinary people) had to respect the upper classes.

- There was a lot of **political conflict**, including plots against the rulers.

- **Men** had far more power than women.

- People were very **religious** and **superstitious**. They believed in witches and magic.

Top Tip!

Learn about Shakespeare and his world to get a better understanding of your play – but don't write about these facts in the test unless they are relevant to the question and the set scenes.

The theatre

- The theatre was very **popular** in Shakespeare's day – people had no TV or cinema. Rich and poor all watched his plays.

- **Stage** and **scenery** were very simple. There were many rough and ready outdoor productions.

- Plays are divided into **acts**. Each act has one or more **scenes**. They include dialogue and stage directions.

This extract from *The Tempest* shows some key features of Shakespeare's plays.

Act 1 Scene 1

On a ship at sea. A tempestuous noise of thunder and lightning heard.
Enter a Shipmaster and a Boatswain severally

MASTER   Boatswain!
BOATSWAIN   Here, master: what cheer?
MASTER   Good, speak to the mariners: fall to't yarely, or we run ourselves aground: bestir, bestir.   *[Exit]*

Enter Mariners

BOATSWAIN   Heigh, my hearts! cheerly, cheerly, my hearts! yare, yare! Take in the topsail. Tend to the master's whistle.
Blow, till thou burst thy wind, if room enough!

This is the **opening scene** of the play. The dramatic start would help to quiet the crowds.

The **setting** is given at the start of each scene.

The **character's name** is in capitals. It is followed by their **lines** (what they say).

Stage directions. Exit = leaves the stage

Scenery, etc. was very basic, so the audience needs to be **told exactly what is happening**.

Did You Know?

Women were not allowed to act in Shakespeare's day, so boys played all the female roles.

Spot Check

1 What is a history play?
2 Give two differences between the theatre in Shakespeare's time and today.
3 Give one feature of Shakespeare's comedies.

Different kinds of language

- Most of the lines are in **verse** (usually not rhymed). Each line has a regular pattern of **10 syllables**, with emphasis on every other syllable:
  Go, <u>charge</u> my <u>gob</u>lins <u>that</u> they <u>grind</u> their <u>joints</u>

- Some passages are in **prose** (ordinary writing), especially when comic characters and the lower classes are speaking:
  What have we here? a man or a fish? dead or alive? A fish: he smells like a fish …

- **Long speeches** are often full of expression and feeling.

- Characters often speak **alternate lines** when they are arguing.

Expressive language

- Shakespeare uses **striking vocabulary** (choice of words):
  – to show a character's **feelings**, e.g. *underhand corrupted foul injustice* (Buckingham about Richard's government, in *Richard III*).
  – to draw a vivid **picture**, e.g. *plunged in the foaming brine* (Ariel about the shipwreck, in *The Tempest*).

- He also **plays with words**, especially in comic scenes:
  Though thou canst swim like a duck, thou art made like a goose (Stephano about Trinculo, in *The Tempest*).

- **Sound effects** such as **alliteration** (repeated sounds) add power to the poetry, e.g. *To take her in her heart's extremest hate* (*Richard III*).

- **Imagery** creates word pictures in the minds of the audience:
  – **similes**: *as chaste as is the bud ere it be blown* (*Much Ado About Nothing*)
  – **metaphors**: *that bottled spider who's deadly web ensnareth thee about* (Margaret about Richard, in *Richard III*)
  – **personification**: *The winds did sing it to me, and the thunder* (*The Tempest*)

Strange language

Shakespeare's language is 400 years old and very poetic. It includes:

- **old-fashioned words**, e.g. *thee/thou* (= you), *thy* (= your), *hath/hast* (= has)

- **strange word order**, e.g. *Thee of thy son, Alonso, they have bereft* (= They have taken your son away from you, Alonso.)

- **missing letters**, e.g. *'scape* = escape, *shak'd* = shaked (shook). Note that *shak'd* is pronounced as one syllable, *shaked* as two syllables.

> **Top Tip!**
>
> **Reading the script aloud**, slowly, will help you to understand it. Do not pause at the end of the lines unless there is a comma or full stop.

Example

The spirit Ariel describes how he casts a spell on the drunken Caliban and his friends (*The Tempest*, Act 4 Scene 1).
Note:

- the **similes** – he compares them first to young horses (colts), then to calves following the sound of the herd
- the **vivid description** of the scene.

> Then I beat my tabor*,
> At which, like unback'd* colts, they prick'd their ears,
> Advanc'd their eyelids, lifted up their noses
> As they smelt music: so I charm'd their ears
> That, calf-like, they my lowing follow'd* through
> Tooth'd briers, sharp furzes, pricking goss and thorns*,
> Which enter'd their frail shins.

*drum

*not yet ridden

*they followed my 'mooing'

*all are prickly plants

Did You Know?

Many common expressions first appeared in Shakespeare's works, including 'love letter', 'puppy dog', 'wild goose chase' and 'what the dickens'.

Spot Check

1 When does Shakespeare use prose?
2 What is alliteration?
3 What is their guilt compared to in this simile from *The Tempest*?
their great guilt, like poison given to work a great time after, now 'gins to bite the spirits

Planning your answer

Spend the first 10 minutes planning your answer. Here is a good way to do it:

1 Make sure you understand the question

Think carefully about what the question is asking you to do. Look at these questions, for example:

How does Caliban's language show his feelings for Prospero?

This question is about Shakespeare's **language**. The focus is on **Caliban's feelings** for Prospero, in *The Tempest*.

Top Tip!

Your essay needs to be **balanced**, so make sure you cover **all the scenes** in your planning.

What problems would the director have to solve in putting on these scenes?

This question is about **performing** the play. The focus is on **problems** in performance.

What different impressions of Richard do we get in these extracts?

This question is about the **character** of Richard III. The focus is on the **different sides** of his character, including **why** he behaves as he does.

2 Re-read the extracts

- Read the extracts again, **with the question in mind**.

- **Highlight the key words** or passages that relate to the question.

3 Brainstorm ideas

- Jot down some **key words** or **ideas**, and add some **quotations** next to them. Use a spider diagram or other planning tool to help you:

What impressions do we get of Richard in Act 1 Scene 1 and Act 4 Scene 2?

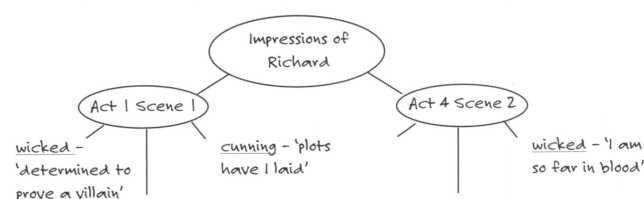

- Use this as the **plan** for your answer.

- Decide on the **order** in which you will discuss each main point.

Example

Here is a completed plan (using a different planning tool) to answer the question:

What impressions do we get of Richard in Act 1 Scene 1 and Act 4 Scene 2?

<u>Intro</u>	both scenes are key for R's character
<u>Act 1 Scene 1</u>	
sly	'imprisonment shall not be long' (to Clarence)
wicked	'determined to prove a villain'
angry about being deformed	'cheated of feature'
cunning	'plots have I laid'
<u>Act 4 Scene 2</u>	
ruthless	wants to kill princes
	'tear-falling pity dwells not'
angry	Buckingham won't obey him
wicked	'I am so far in blood'
cunning	wants to spread rumours about his wife
<u>Conclusion</u>	just as bad and cunning later in play,
	but losing control, getting desperate

Did You Know?

The 'Reduced Shakespeare' theatre company have summarised all 37 of Shakespeare's plays and turned them into one fast-moving comedy lasting an hour and a half.

Spot Check

What are these questions asking you to focus on? Match each question with a focus.

Questions

1 Explain whether you think Caliban is foolish in these scenes.

2 How do Ferdinand and Miranda show in their words that they are deeply in love?

3 What advice would you give the actor playing Ariel in these scenes?

Focus of the question

a language

b performance

c character

Begin and end effectively

- Begin with an **introduction**. This should show that you **understand the question**, by referring to key words. Do not give details at this point, e.g.
  Caliban shows several different feelings in these scenes.

- End with a **conclusion**. This should summarise the key points, e.g.
  So we have seen that Caliban's feelings are wide-ranging. First he is …

Top Tip!

For each main point that you make in your answer, give a quotation from the extracts and explain why it is relevant (**Point – Evidence – Comment**). This shows the examiners that you are basing your ideas on the play, and that you understand the play.

Refer to the extracts

You must always refer to the extracts to back up your points. Use one of these methods for each point:

- **Summarise** the evidence in your own words, e.g.
  Antonio suggests a brutal plot to murder the sleeping king.

- Include **short quotations** in your sentences. Remember to use quote marks, e.g.
  In a powerful image, Ariel describes Ferdinand's hair as standing up 'like reeds'.

- Separate **longer quotations** from your text, leaving a line space before and after. Don't include more than one or two long quotations. The examiners want to see your own ideas and your own words.

Remember: **Point – Evidence – Comment**. Begin by making your own point, in your own words. Then quote from the extract to back up your point. Finally, use your own words to explain how the quotation backs up your point.

Page 83.

Write well

- **Write clearly**. Use one paragraph per point. Use words to link your ideas, e.g. *in addition, by contrast, also, however.*

- Try to **develop each point** rather than giving one straightforward fact each time.

This is the beginning of an answer to the question:

How does Shakespeare make the audience laugh in Act 2 Scene 2 and Act 3 Scene 2 of *The Tempest*?

Introduction shows student understands the question and refers to the key points briefly.

There are all sorts of skills in these scenes to make the audience laugh. The characters are funny, there is a lot of slapstick and misunderstanding as well.

To begin with Caliban thinks that Trinculo is a spirit who Prospero sends to torment him. This is funny as Trinculo is only a jester. Caliban keeps making this mistake for a long time which is funny. So after Stephano sings, Caliban says 'Do not torment me: O!' and he says it again later. Every time Caliban says this, it makes the audience laugh.

Evidence is summarised in student's own words. A **comment** is still given.

Point – misunderstanding is kept going.
Evidence – 'Do not torment me: O!'
Comment – why it is effective.

One **paragraph** used for this main point.
Language is clear.

Stephano forces Caliban to drink while Trinculo hides under the covers (from Act 2 Scene 2, *The Tempest*). This photograph is from a modern interpretation performed by the Royal Shakespeare Company.

Did You Know?
You can rearrange the letters in 'William Shakespeare' to make 'I am a weakish speller'.

Spot Check

1 Explain what an introduction should do.
2 Why should you quote directly from the extracts?
3 What does the phrase 'Point – Evidence – Comment' help you to remember?

Revising for questions on characters

You may be asked to describe how a character behaves in the set scenes. Here is how to make sure you are ready for a question like this:

- **Make a character log** for the characters in your play, with brief descriptions of who they are. Some of this could be in the form of a family tree, e.g.

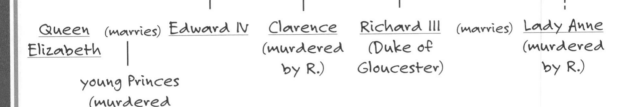

Duchess of York
mother of :

| Queen Elizabeth | (marries) | Edward IV | Clarence (murdered by R.) | Richard III (Duke of Gloucester) | (marries) | Lady Anne (murdered by R.) |

young Princes (murdered by R.)

Queen Margaret (mother-in-law of Lady Anne)

- Take two or three of the main characters and compile a **spider diagram of their key qualities**, e.g.

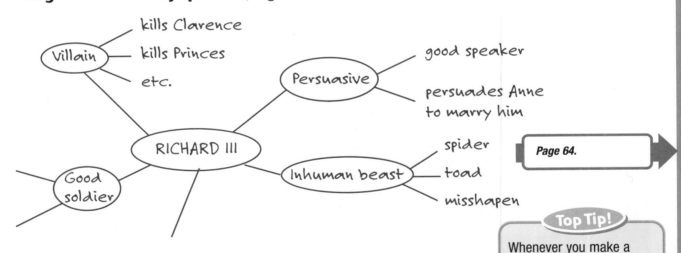

Villain — kills Clarence, kills Princes, etc.

Persuasive — good speaker, persuades Anne to marry him

RICHARD III

Good soldier

Inhuman beast — spider, toad, misshapen

Page 64.

Top Tip!
Whenever you make a point about a character, back it up with a quotation from the extracts.

Describing a character

When describing what a character is like, refer to:

- **what they say,** e.g. *Caliban acts like a slave. He says, 'I will kiss thy foot.'*

- **what they do,** e.g. *Caliban shows Prospero 'all the qualities o' th' isle'.*

- **what others say about them,** e.g. *Trinculo calls him 'a most ridiculous monster'.*

- **why they behave as they do,** e.g. *Caliban wanted to kill Prospero so that he could live on his island as a free man.*

Did You Know?
The largest speaking part in all of Shakespeare's plays is Hamlet (nearly 1500 lines).

Occasionally you are asked to write as if you were one of the characters of the play. This means you have to:

- **imagine what it feels** like to be them in that situation.

- **stay in role** – refer to yourself throughout as 'I' and 'me' and keep that pretence going.

- **explain** what you are doing, thinking and feeling and why.

- **quote** from the set scenes to back up what you say.

Example

This is the start of a level 5 answer to the question:

level 5

What impressions do we get of Benedick in Act 1 Scene 1 and Act 2 Scene 3 of *Much Ado About Nothing*?

Note the **good points**, and the **things that need improving**.

> In the first scene Benedick gives the impression of someone who thinks he is quite funny and is always making jokes. When he's asked what Hero is like he says, 'I can see without spectacles'. This means he doesn't need help to look at women.
>
> But Benedick is also quite arrogant – he says women and love aren't at all important to him. For example, he argues with his boss Don Pedro:
>
> Don Pedro: I shall see thee, ere I die, look pale with love.
>
> Benedick: With anger, with sickness, or with hunger, my lord, not with love

First paragraph uses the key word 'impression'… ✓
… but isn't really an introduction to the answer. ✗

Commenting on what Benedick says … ✓
… but it isn't really a joke. ✗

Explains the quotation. ✓

New paragraph for a new point. ✓

Quotation given to back up point … ✓
… but there is too much quotation and not enough explanation. ✗

**pot Check**   Choose one of the main characters in your play. Draw up a spider diagram to display his or her key features or qualities.

Answering questions on ideas and themes

Knowing the story

- You won't be asked to discuss the **plot** (the story of the whole play), but you do need to know about it. Draw up a **storyline** to remind yourself, like this one about *The Tempest*:

> Act 1   The shipwreck
>
> Prospero tells Miranda about his past
>
> The history of the spirit Ariel is described
>
> Prospero and Miranda visit Caliban

Themes

The themes of a play are the **main ideas** it explores. You could be asked to discuss how a single theme is explored in the extracts.

The Tempest
- **forgiveness** – Prospero and his enemies, Caliban and Prospero
- **master and servant** – Caliban/Ariel and Prospero, Gonzalo and Alonso
- **magic** – Prospero a 'good' magician, Ariel a spirit

Much Ado About Nothing
- **love and marriage** – Benedick and Beatrice, Hero and Claudio
- **tricks and deception** – e.g. Benedick is tricked to make him fall in love
- **role of women** – Beatrice is powerless as a woman, daughters ruled by fathers

Top Tip!

If you are asked about a theme, don't talk in general about it but relate it to the scenes provided. Remember to back up your ideas with quotes from the extracts.

Richard III
- **hatred and evil** – Richard is full of both, but fascinating to the audience
- **blame and guilt** – blames others for misfortunes and guilty conscience for killings
- **deception** – Richard deceives Buckingham, Clarence, Anne, Hastings

Preparing for a question on theme

- Draw up a spider diagram for each theme of your play. Add detail as you study it, e.g.

Prospero a 'good' witch – uses powers to serve good

brings Ferdinand and Miranda together

arranges for a reconciliation with Antonio

Magic in 'The Tempest'

Caliban's mother Sycorax a 'bad' witch

Ariel a spirit with magic powers

Context – people believed in magic
—James I wrote about witchcraft

Example

This is the start of a level 5 answer to the question:

What different ideas about women are explored in Act 1 Scene 1 and Act 2 Scene 3 of *Much Ado About Nothing*?

Note the **good points**, and **the things that need improving**.

level 5

In the first scene, women are mostly seen as something to have a bit of a laugh about. Benedick is proud of being nasty to women, and he's not very nice about Hero. But he does compliment Beatrice, saying:

'There's her cousin, and she were not possessed of a fury, exceeds her as much in beauty as the first of May doth the last of December'.

There is a lot of talk about how women look. They have to be 'fair' and 'modest'. It's like they aren't allowed to be witty and clever – only the men can be that.

Needs an **introduction**. ✗

First point made clearly … ✓
… but needs backing up with quote and comment. ✗

Quotation used to back up point … ✓
… but it isn't explained or commented on. ✗

New paragraph for a new point. ✓

Throughout the focus is on **ideas about women** in the two **scenes** given. ✓

 **Spot Check**

Draw up a spider diagram for one of the main themes of your play. Show how the theme is explored in different scenes and by different characters.

Questions on language

- You may be asked to focus on the language used in the set scenes, e.g.

  How does Caliban's language show that he is fearful ...?

  How do the characters use language to battle with each other ...?

  How does Shakespeare build up a mood of tension ...?

- In these questions, you need to explain what the language shows, and **what effect** it has.

What the language shows

- Think about what the language is actually saying. Each sentence will have a **purpose**, which could include:
  - to persuade
  - to flatter
  - to deceive
  - to hurt
  - to fill in the background for the audience.

- When commenting on a sentence, **explain** what its purpose is, e.g.
  - Buckingham reflects bitterly on how he has been treated when he says, 'Repays he my deep service with such contempt?'
  - Ariel asks, 'Was't well done?' because he is trying to gain Prospero's favour so that he can be freed.

Top Tip!

Remember to use Point – Evidence – Comment:

Sebastian is so amazed. 'Now I will believe that there are unicorns'. ✗

Sebastian is amazed at the magic. He says, 'Now I will believe that there are unicorns' because unicorns were fabulous beasts that never existed. That shows how fabulous the sight has been. ✓

What effect the language has

- You also need to comment on **how well** the language performs its purpose. Focus on Shakespeare's **expressive language**:

Pages 78–9.

  - **imagery**, e.g. *Margaret's description of Richard as a 'bottled spider' is very accurate, as he lures his victims into his web of deceit.*

  - **powerful words**, e.g. *Buckingham emphasises how bad Richard's government is by piling up the adjectives: 'underhand corrupted foul injustice'.*

  - **sound effects**, e.g. *Caliban almost spits his curse on Prospero (note the repeated 's' sounds): 'all the infections that the sun sucks up'.*

This is the start of a level 5 answer to the question:

Comment on the purpose and effect of these lines from Act 1 Scene 1 of *Richard III*.

level
5

Now are our brows bound with victorious wreaths;
Our bruised arms hung up for monuments;
Our stern alarums changed to merry meetings,
Our dreadful marches to delightful measures.

Note the **good points** and the **things that need improving**.

> In this opening scene of the play Richard is telling the audience that the war in England has ended. He does this in a very descriptive way.
>
> These four lines show a very effective contrast between war and peace. Things to do with war are listed in the first half of each line, and things to do with peace in the second half.
>
> There are lots of repeated sounds, for examples the 'd's and 'm's in 'dreadful marches to delightful measures' (which means dances). The actor would emphasise these sounds for added effect. The repetition of 'Our' at the start of the lines is another powerful sound effect.

The **purpose** of the language is given ... ✓
... but it could say more about why it is so descriptive – because Richard is a persuasive speaker, and to entertain the audience. ✗

The **effect** of the language is commented on ... ✓
... but we need an example of it, such as 'stern alarums have been changed to merry meetings'. A comment could add, 'This is effective because both things relate to noise'. ✗

Effective use of **quotation** here: point – evidence – comment. ✓

Did You Know?

Some of Shakespeare's plays are written completely in verse, such as *King John, Richard II* and *Henry VI Part 1*.

Answering questions on performance

In the director's chair

The question may ask you to **imagine that you are directing** the set scenes, e.g.

What advice would you give to the actor playing Richard?

How would you direct the scene to bring out the conflict between the lovers?

- As a director, you need to think about these aspects of the performance:
  - most importantly, the **acting** – how the actors say their lines, move about the stage and relate to other characters
  - the **set** and **costume design**, **lighting** and **sound**.

Answering the question

- You must **explain** why you are directing in a particular way. That means understanding what the characters are doing and why, e.g.
  He should sink to the ground at this point. ✗
  He is in complete despair, so he should sink to the ground at this point. ✓

- You must **link your ideas with the text** by quoting, e.g.
  When Claudio says 'She is the sweetest lady' he should put his hand on his heart to show how much love he feels.

Focus on character and mood

- Bring out the **feelings** or **key features** of the character in your direction, e.g.
  To show her <u>disgust</u> with Richard, Anne should push him away with her words 'Foul devil'.

- **Emphasise** a particular **mood** by varying the voice, or pace, or adding pauses, e.g.
  Richard should have a <u>fixed smile</u> while saying 'and seem a saint', then <u>pause</u> and say 'when most I play the devil' with a <u>snarl</u>.

> **Top Tip!**
> Imagine the actors on stage as they say their lines. How can movement or feeling really bring out the meaning of their words?

Here is part of a level 5 answer to the question:

How would you direct Caliban in *The Tempest* Act 1 Scene 2 to bring out his relationship with Prospero?

level
5

> Caliban should run onto the stage, hurling his curse at Prospero. He should be defiant when he says 'This island's mine'. He should point accusingly at Prospero at 'Which thou takest from me'. This will underline how angry he feels with Prospero at losing his freedom.

how Caliban should move and speak

point of direction

evidence (quoted)

comment, explaining the direction

Prospero and Caliban threaten and curse each other vehemently (Act 1 Scene 2, *The Tempest*).

Did You Know?

Shakespeare knew how to write for actors because he was an actor as well as a playwright.

Spot Check

True or false?
1 When you are asked to be a director, you have to put on a performance.
2 You don't have to describe how the scenes would have been performed in Shakespeare's day.
3 You can include thoughts on the best lighting and sound.
4 You don't have to quote from the extracts in this kind of

To raise your level from level 4 to level 5 in the Shakespeare paper, follow these guidelines.

Show your understanding

- Show that you really understand the characters, especially **why** they are behaving as they are, e.g.
  Caliban is angry because he used to be free and now he is Prospero's slave.
  Richard is unhappy because Buckingham won't help him murder the Princes.

- Show that you know **how language is used to create an effect.**
  Comment on words and phrases that tell us what a character is feeling or thinking, or what impact Shakespeare is trying to make, e.g.
  The phrase 'great master' shows how much Ariel is a slave to Prospero.
  The Princes are described as 'four red roses on a stalk', which contrasts with the 'ruthless butchery' that Richard is planning.

Quote effectively

- Quote from the extracts frequently, but only to **back up your points**. The quotes must be relevant to the point you are making.

- Short quotations are better than long ones, e.g.
  Caliban reassures them that the noises on the island are harmless:

  > *Be not afeard: the isle is full of noises,*
  > *Sounds and sweet airs, that give delight, and hurt not.*
  > *Sometimes a thousand twangling instruments*
  > *Will hum about mine ears* ✗

  Caliban reassures them that the noises on the island are harmless ('hurt not'). ✓

- Give a **comment** explaining why the quotation makes your point, e.g.
  Richard blames Anne for the murders: 'Your beauty was the cause of that effect: Your beauty ...'. The repeated words 'your beauty' make her responsible for what happened.

Top Tip!

Only tell the story of the scene if it is relevant to the point you are making.

Look at the beginning of this level 5 answer to the question:

What impressions do we get of Richard in Act 1 Scene 1 and Act 3 Scene 7?

level
5

In the first scene the impression we get of Richard is of someone who loves talking about himself and what he can do. But he is also unhappy that he is ugly: 'he is cheated of feature by dissembling nature'. Because of his appearance and because he doesn't like the 'sportive tricks' of peace time, he decides to follow evil: 'I am determined to prove a villain'. This is the main impression we get of Richard, that he is evil.

Richard comes across as 'subtle, false and treacherous', because he is laying plots everywhere. The three words build up a clear picture of how deceitful he is. He is even plotting against his brother.

No introduction, but answer refers immediately to the key word 'impression'.

Focus throughout is on impressions of Richard – answer shows his character is understood.

Notes how language creates an effect and adds a comment on the quotation.

Did You Know?

William Shakespeare had eleven different ways of spelling his name.

Glossary

adjective   a describing word, e.g. 'red', 'evil'

advice   a text type which has the aim of suggesting a course of action

alliteration   the effect created when words next to each other begin with the same letter (e.g. 'terrible twins')

analyse   to investigate something carefully and thoroughly

apostrophe   a punctuation mark used to show either possession (e.g. 'Dave's computer') or a missing letter (e.g. 'can't')

argument   a text type which presents and develops a particular point of view

audience   someone who listens to or reads a text

bias   weighting a text unfairly in favour of one side or the other

blank verse   in Shakespeare's plays, unrhymed verse with 10 syllables in each line

characterisation   how an author presents and develops their characters

clause   a group of words in a sentence which expresses a single idea; a clause has a verb and usually a subject

colon   a punctuation mark that introduces a clause which leads on from or explains another clause

comedy   a Shakespearean play about relationships with a happy ending

command   a verb that gives an instruction to the reader, e.g. '<u>Think</u> about your children …'

complex sentence   a sentence with one main clause and one or more subordinate clauses

compound sentence   a sentence made up of two or more simple sentences linked by 'and', 'but' or 'or'

connective   a word or phrase which links clauses and sentences, to signal to the audience where the text is going

direct address   using the second person ('you') to hold the reader's attention in a text

discussion   a text type which helps the audience understand an issue by presenting the different viewpoints fairly

emotive language   words, phrases and ideas designed to make the audience feel something strongly

explanation   a text type which helps the audience understand why or how something is as it is

fact   a piece of knowledge or information that can be proved to be true

fiction   anything that is made up, especially a story

formal language   writing or speech that follows the strictest rules of Standard English

homophone   a word that sounds the same as another but is spelt differently, e.g. 'where' and 'wear'

imagery   the use of language to create an image or picture; *see also* simile, metaphor, personification

informal language   language that does not follow the strict rules of Standard English

information   a text type which presents facts in a way that is easy to understand

instruction   a text type which tells the audience how to do something, through a series of sequenced steps

inverted comma   a punctuation mark used to show the beginning and end of direct speech

media   the term given to texts aimed at large numbers of people, e.g. television, magazines, newspapers, Internet

metaphor   a type of imagery which describes something as something else, e.g. 'you are an island'

motivation   why a character behaves as he or she does

non-fiction   any text that is not made up

opinion   a person's own view about something

paragraph   a group of sentences on one topic, person or event. A new paragraph begins a new line.

paraphrase   to summarise part of the text in your own words

person   a way of referring to pronouns and verbs according to whether they indicate the speaker/writer (1st person: 'I', 'we'), the audience (2nd person: 'you') or someone else (3rd person: 's/he', 'it', 'they')

personification   a type of imagery which refers to objects as if they were human, e.g. 'the sun punished them'

persuasion   a text type which has the aim of selling an idea or a product

phrase   a group of words which go together, e.g. 'the garden gate'

plot   the storyline

popular newspaper   a newspaper that aims to entertain as much as to inform its readers, e.g. *The Sun, The Mirror*

prefix   letters added at the start of a word to change its meaning

punctuation   a way of marking text with symbols to make the meaning clear

purpose   the aim of a text

recount   a text type which tells the reader what happened, often in an informative and entertaining way

relative clause   part of the sentence beginning 'who', 'which', 'that' etc. which gives more information about the main clause

rhetorical question   a question asked for effect, not for an answer

rhetorical technique   a technique used to persuade an audience, e.g. emotive language, sound effects, repetition, rhetorical questions

romance   a Shakespearean play that mixes elements of tragedy and comedy

scan   to look over a text quickly in order to find a particular word or piece of information

semi-colon   a punctuation mark used to show a pause in a sentence longer than a comma

simile   a type of imagery which compares something with something else, making the comparison clear by using a phrase such as 'like; or 'as if', e.g. 'she swam like a fish'

simple sentence   a sentences with only one clause

skim   to read a whole text quickly

slogan   a memorable phrase used to sell a product

Standard English   the type of spoken and written English that is generally considered 'correct' and that is taught in schools

suffix   letters added at the end of a word to change its meaning

summarise   to identify the key points of a text

text   a block of spoken or written language

theme   the underlying ideas or issues that a story or play deals with

tone   a measure of the quality, mood or style of a piece of writing

topic sentence   the main sentence in a paragraph, which gives the topic (subject) of the paragraph

tragedy   a Shakespearean play with an unhappy ending

verb   a word that refers to an action, e.g. 'runs' or a state of being, e.g. 'feels'

Index